Fake News and The New Social Media

Date of the on-line conference:

September 26th-27th, 2022

Editors:

Roman Lindauer, Dipl. Mgmt.

Mgr. Tereza Kubankova

Publisher:

ISBN: 978-0-9996639-3-6

Reference:

Lindauer, R. & Kubankova, T. (Eds.). (2022). Fake News and The New Social Media, LIGS University. ISBN: 978-0-9996639-2-9

About LIGS University

The Mission of LIGS University is to provide high-quality, affordable, and state-of-the-art education using innovative delivery technologies for diverse students all over the world.

The Vision of LIGS University is to be a high-quality, innovative educational institution providing services that significantly surpass the expectations of students, faculty, and other stakeholders. The vision of LIGS University is to commit to achieving our core values for which the acronym LIGS stands for.

Leadership
Innovation
Growth
Success

Partner

EDU Effective

EDU Effective is an educational institution offering **joint programs** bringing together the best of American (EDU Effective Business School US) and European (EDU Effective EU) professional degree programs. In highly practical and **up-to-date online education,** you can learn from the **best leaders** in the industry in **flexible 15 min classes** to gain a clear understanding to boost your professional career or launch and scale your own business.

President's Message

In our current world, the issue of "fake news" has grown to epidemic proportion, much like Covid-19 had. While many may absorb the news without questions- these people will inevitably become confused and misguided. Think of the consequences: how we support our leaders, how we manage our local communities, work environments, social groups. It is certainly possible that we could be falsely influenced into making incorrect or inappropriate decision in many important areas of our lives. The need to separate out the truth from the "spin' on a topic has never been more in demand. Why do we have "fake news" in the first place? Could it be that the various new outlets are driven by ratings and revenue, drama. Viewership, over truthful news reporting. It has become a real challenge to fine unbiased and factual reporting. It certainly is out there; however often overshadowed by these disingenuous news outlets that value revenue/money over truthful and unfiltered news.

The time is "now" for all of us to exercise critical thinking and analysis to decipher the information and to separate out fact from fiction. While not easy to do, it is necessary for us to carefully understand the rhetoric and the reality. The ability to comprehensively understand the facts is becoming part of our everyday decision processes and so very important to ourselves and communities.

We need to be a clear minded community when considering how we support our local, national, and global leaders. Times are certainly now easier and decisions are becoming much tougher. This alone calls for dedicated review of important topics- free from fake news and twisted reporting. Free to decide our futures free from biased influence and distortion. We certainly have enough challenges facing us, regardless of our home countries and neighborhoods. As decisions become more and more important; any negative components of the decision process will undoubtably hinder future growth, happiness, and progress.

If we all stopped listening to the "fake news" providers; would it go away? This is tough to answer- but maybe worth a try. Of course, figuring out the fake news from the reality is the first major task to complete. This is where our critical thinking and analysis skills come into play.

Hopefully, we can all learn from a better understanding of the dire consequences of fake news that is flooding our news channels.

Dr. William A. Reed

President of LIGS University

Table of Contents

About LIGS University 4

President's Message
William A. Reed 6

Conference Keynote Speech
Roman Lindauer 11

Fake News and New Social Media: The phenomenon from several viewpoints
Nnenna Uboma 16

Fake News and New Social Media: Ghana's Legal Response
Dennis Owusu-Appiah Ofosuapea 47

The Battle of Fake News in Social Media: Case of Political Elections in Indonesia
Richardus Eko Indrajit 63

Fake News and the New Social Media: The perception of youth on implication and possible solution
Suwaiba Muhammad Dankabo 77

Healthcare text generated by AI has the potential to misinform and not be recognized as AI content by either healthcare professionals or the general public
Natalie Bourré 91

Fake News and New Social Media and the Impact on Women Entrepreneurship
Carolina M. Billings 108

Exploring weaknesses in Facebook's algorithm and Cambridge Analytica
Jiri Medlen, Patrick Medlen, Lenka Sulova 132

Did Fake News on Facebook Influence Electoral and Health Decisions?
Laura McCoy 157

The Art of Fake News Creation and Dissemination
Jiri Medlen, Patrick Medlen 174

Exploring Covid-19 Conspiracy Theories in Nigeria
Reuben Ufot Etuk 199

Conference Keynote Speech

For more than 25 years, we all are living in the era of internet. This amazing technological tool changes our viewpoints on news, their distribution, correctness and acceptance. The global users of internet can search for information, they can comment of discuss any topic with no limitation as censorship or access to the traditional media channels.

Internet becomes a constant part of our lives and many millions of people every day are consuming terabytes of various news and available information. As much the number of users increased, the same way increased the news, which are not fully true. In other words, we are confronting with the fake news. We may see how some people started to manipulate with the initial substance of the news to make it highly effective munition in the time of information war. Information, which are spreading through current fast communication channels across the globe, are in most cases shared very quickly among the target population. Some internet users have ambition to bend the reality to deliver a better picture about some situation or influence the public opinion. These tendencies are also called the fake news.

Fake news is the news that were fabricated with the bad will by someone. Fake news using the expressive language or presenting facts in a shocking way. Fake news is easy to spot, easy to read and understand for anyone. Fake news as truly global phenomenon will not fade out very soon. The questionable value of the fake news would be connected with the negative impact, which may have on the recipients of such fake news.

We may ask whom are the people preparing the fake news? Who orders the fake news? By which reason? Who may benefit from their existence? These questions have no clear answers but we will never stop asking.

We presume the majority of the internet news are relatively correct so the total volume of the fake news represents just a small part of the total global news coverage. This ratio still represents a huge room for manipulations, spreading fear and uncertainty. The danger is the fake news may grow up and start the uncontrollable snowball effect which might be devastating for democracy and freedom of speech if we won't be aware about this danger.

Nowadays are still existing the traditional institutions which presenting the news not spoiled by any manipulation to the global audience. These institutions are standing opposite to the many local or regional centers that are in the hands of the people who may have an intention to present the fake reality to the local communities.

Good example of such trends is the fake news, which were very popular on the beginning of the Covid19 pandemic. Nearly every day was possible to read various news who may be responsible for spreading the Covid19. During the complicated time when people are confronting with the unknown danger, they are likely to accept easy answers presenting them in the easy consumable way.

With the advancement of the artificial intelligence the fake news will be automatically generated after the entering the theme and degree of cruelty. The machinery of such fake news might be very unpredictable. There is a probability after some time there will be no difference in the language of style when comparing the regular news and fake news. Internet wiped out the traditional borders and we have no more excuses because we are confronting with the same or similar fake news every day

I personally believe the incorporation of ethical principles into the news legislation can be tool, which can eliminate the fake news. The spread of false or unauthorized information will be, a criminal act and organizations uncompliant with these principles will be charged by penalties.

It is obvious the fake news was always present in the oral tradition of the humankind. Just modern technologies accelerated the speed of their circulation around the globe and number of potential recipients.

We need to find our own ways, how to detect, eliminate and suppress the fake news. As the industrial smog is unacceptable may come the time when fake news will be also unacceptable in a normal decent society.

During our conference, our speakers will present several excellent papers describing the negative face of the fake news. They will present the real cases like the implication of the fake news to the young people, how the fake news may be use during the political battles, where lies the roots of the fake news and their consequences, the relation between the fake news and new social media, how the fake news could be criminalized, the technical analyses of Facebook and Cambridge Analytica from the viewpoint of Brexit voting and other topics.

Their ambition was to explain the fake news and their potential impact on the society. How to tackle with the fake news will be a subject of next two days. I am sure we will try at least to get find a solution.

Please enjoy the 4th LIGS University on-line conference on the topic of fake news.

Roman Lindauer, Dipl. Mgmt.

Member of LIGS University Faculty

& Conference Supervisor

Fake News and New Social Media: The phenomenon from several viewpoints.

Nnenna Uboma

Abstract

Most of the decision-makers in conventional media are nameless and anonymous, and they determine what is printed and transmitted and what is not. The way that news and information are produced and consumed in modern society is evolving in this new internet age with its array of social media. A recent development is the quick conversion of traditional print media to web portals. Online social media has on the one hand made news production and distribution more accessible, but on the other, it has also transformed into a platform for deception and fake news. The popularity of mobile devices and the ease of connecting Wi-Fi to 3G/4G networks have made social media sites like Facebook, Instagram, YouTube, and Twitter into effective venues for information acquirement and entertainment. The US political leaders including the President use Twitter to interact with their constituents and followers. The use of social media by politicians and other decision-makers to communicate directly with the public significantly impact how the world governments are run. Online journalism and citizen media are therefore expanding as well. New internet communication methods like WhatsApp, Messenger, Skype, and many others have greatly increased the broadcast of false material. This research uses a substantive literature review to examine the present problems with fake news. Findings from the research indicate that fake news through the new social media is realistic and much attention should be made to suppress the negative societal impacts it has at any time. With the necessary intervention measures in place there is likelihood of allowing society to acquire only the information relevant to them.

Keywords: *social media, Fake news, Social bots, Channels, Distribution, Internet, False information*

JEL Classification: *I1, I2, I3*

Introduction

The rapid spread of fake news, resulting from the social media trend, calls for scrutiny and action. Fake news is not a strange spectacle, but it has lately drawn a much responsiveness due to the extensive use of new social media for communication as well as for the dissemination of news and ideas. According to Warner-Sderholm et al. (2018), social media is the "lifeline of fake news" because it makes it easy for anyone to spread a false tale that goes viral. With social media's widespread use and the simplicity with which information can be shared thanks to its technological capabilities, there is concern regarding the proliferation of fake news. The negative impact cannot be ignored, considering the new social media platforms increase the opportunity to express propaganda.

According to Quandt (2019), social media platforms encourage the propagation of problematic news information and allow for its circulation in a unique, baffling manner. Additionally, because of the speed at which news content travels on social media, fake news spreads quickly and is difficult to stop. Thus, the spread of fake news has driven attention on a global scale. Even if fake news is a problem everywhere, it is frequently attracted by regional problems and specific circumstances. A motive typology derived from the great majority of Western-centric studies may not adequately reflect cultural characteristics influencing why people disseminate news or fake news, for instance. The effects of fake news circulating through society might vary significantly among different societies. Given the local nature of this global issue, it is crucial to look at the micro-level spread of fake news. This study examines earlier research on fake news in the US to offer a microanalysis of the causes or motivations for disseminating false information in the US and its effects on the public.

Problem Statement

According to Motsaathebe (2011) the news media is typically recognized as a reliable source of a genuine account of events worldwide. Journalists use a variety of sources when reporting the news to confirm or provide credibility to the content they present. Kolawole (2017) further indicated that fake news is becoming the greatest thing in society especially in the era where social media has escalated in use.

The art of fabricating articles from one's comfort zone because of possessing a smartphone with an inexpensive connection is becoming increasingly popular. Although social media was not invented in the current generation, there has been prolific use, and the impact continues to grow even further. For most people's lives, there is exposure to fake news. For instance, false information in the '#pizzagate" hashtag led to riots in the US. The aforementioned claims highlight how fake news disturbs not only the media but also society. The problem of fake news is spreading like wildfire, thanks to the development of new media, and its detrimental effects on well-known online newspapers are plain to see.

Literature Review

Mass Media and Social Media Concept

The deteriorating reliance in mainstream media could be both an effect and a concern of fake news acquiring more popularity (Allcot & Gentzkow, 2017). If false news has an influence on traditional newspapers, consider what it will do to large internet publications. Everyone does not totally understand the difference between social media and popular online newspapers. Allcot & Gentzkow (2017) further noted that some people still hold the opinion that there is no distinction between Facebook and a major news website. Considerably, it is criticized that any unfavorable perceptions of one will be shared by the other. Popular online publications are too crucial to the fabric of society to be completely tarnished by what people write on social media. Taking this into account, in addition to the need to maintain the egotism of position previously held by the print newsprint in establishing the issue and, among other duties, maintaining the government answerable to the societies, humanity stands to lose significantly if well-liked online newspapers collapse (Gentzkow, 2017). Nevertheless, social media has imposed a great force where the freedom of expression is more pronounced.

Consequently, technology intended toward a large clientele size is regarded to as mass media. According to Carr & Hayes (2015), the great number of people in the population could be addressed expending it as their primary information delivery tool. Radio, television, magazines, newspapers, and the Internet are the channels for mass media that are used the most frequently. The general population often turns to the media for insight on political matters, health concerns, economic issues, social issues, entertainment, and news. Given the importance of the mainstream media's functions as a social institution Carr & Hayes (2015), further indicated that is not overstating the case to say that their presence is essential to both the functioning of society as a whole and the government and its agencies. This indicates that the mass media has duties intended to maintain society's harmony, cohesion, and development.

However, the mainstream media assigns the task of obtaining and disseminating information to a diverse audience. Allcott et al. (2020) indicated that social media then arose to compliment the mainstream media to deliver information to the various audiences for informational, educational, and entertainment purposes for the general public. The various media forms are responsible for maintaining the values, opinions, and actions that advance social harmony, cohesion, and stability. Wright (1956) identified two key sociological characteristics of the mass media: first, the ability of a small number of persons to communicate with a massive group; and second, the audience's lack of effective means of retaliation. By definition, mass communication is a one-way mechanism. Except in cultures where the government controls the media, media institutions are bureaucratic and professional in nature (Parry & Solidoro, 2013). Governments worldwide oversee media production, although the censorship varies from minimal advisory regulation to the most extreme forms in authoritarian nations.

To effectively deceive the public, fake news is designed to resemble twisted nematic by imitating its qualities such as verifiability, brevity, precision, consistency, and honesty (Han et al., 2017). Burkhardt (2017) reported that fake news has existed since the ancient times, when the first Roman Emperor had to spread false information to persuade Octavian to overthrow the republican system. Since defying authority was considered treason during the Roman era, there was no way to confirm and validate the veracity of the news. News misinformation first appeared in the 20th century with the advent of numerous one-to-many channels of communication like newspapers, radio channels, and television networks (Kim et al., 2020). The composition of fake news has been reaching new consumers thanks to the advent of multimedia organizations and the advent of the Internet enhanced the spectacle of fake news. In the 21st century, as technology developed, SM appeared and multiplied the spread of fake news using both one-to-many and many-to-many techniques.

Security Implications

One of the information security implications of false news has also been called out: data integrity according to Monsees (2020), data is progressively being viewed as a valuable asset in the corporate world today, thus, it is crucial that organizations have all required safeguards in place to prevent unauthorized individuals from accessing sensitive data. However, the presence of content creators who are eager to spread false information renders such attempts useless. In light of this, businesses are spending more money to support the creation and formulation of better solutions that can be applied to combat the consequences of utilizing clickbait to entice consumers to divulge their personal information.

However, despite being warned against it, Aldwairi & Alwahedi (2018) depicted that employees still go to these websites, putting their companies in danger of cyber-attacks. Conversely, some academics contend that false information occasionally has advantageous repercussions. As an illustration, there have been instances where bogus news caused the share prices of publicly traded firms to rise. Aldwairi & Alwahedi (2018) further depicted prospective investors become more interested in the company's operations as more people post the link to the website providing the material that appears to be relevant to it, which, in turn, causes the share price to rise significantly. However, such modifications are sure to have severe effects because most people who purchase shares based on false information end up being dissatisfied.

Consumer Perspectives

Gaozhao (2021) argued that consumers have a variety of prior convictions about how the world is doing. Priors among liberal consumers predict that the candidate with a left-leaning stance would accomplish better outcomes in office, whereas those of conventional consumers predict that the candidate with a right-leaning perspective will work better. The utility is delivered to customers via two channels. They want to find out the truth first. In our concept, customers must decide between endorsing or voting for a candidate, and they gain personal benefit if they select the one they would support if they had all the information. Secondly, viewing congruent reports with their deeper perception may provide consumers with psychological utility. When maximizing their own anticipated utility, consumers choose the companies from which they obtain information. They then opinionate about the world state grounded on the information in the news materials they have read (Chen & Cheng, 2019). Consumers must choose between their own motive to consume accurate and unbiased news and their psychological benefit from confirmatory news.

Chen & Cheng (2019) further indicated that, after making their decisions, customers might then get more information about how the world really is after seeing, for instance, how a candidate performs while in government. Then, consumers choose which media companies to continue consuming and revise their perceptions of their quality. Due to the fact that advertising money increases media companies' revenues, they are motivated to establish a reputation for providing their audience with high levels of utility (Rodríguez et al., 2020). Furthermore, selecting the more qualified individual has advantageous social implications for the buyer.

In a similar spirit, other studies have remarked that fake news can support an organization's marketing goals. For instance, more customers get interested in the products given by a company when the data delivered on the websites related with such news is one that supports that product regardless of whether what is included as the content deviates from reality. (Chiluwa, & Samoilenko, 2019; Aldwairi & Alwahedi, 2018) Even if the fake news was not a part of the organization's marketing campaigns, it nonetheless manages to reach a larger group of potential customers. According to academics, fake news as a notion is not entirely negative because it can help an organization develop. This inclination has limitations, too, and firms should not rely on it because the contrary would have far-reaching adverse effects (Mishra, & Samu, 2021). Even if the information spread to potential consumers was untrue, a company's performance is sure to suffer when the webpage contents hold false material that paints the company in an unfavorable light.

Additionally, Mourão & Robertson (2019) argued that fake news as expansive assimilation after an examination of sites that issue false, deceptive, hyperpartisan and appealing information, it is clear that the concept of utilizing sensationalism to entice unsuspecting visitors to web pages has significantly influenced perceptions in contexts other than those involving the commercial environment. For example, fake news was widely disseminated through social media platforms during the occasions leading up to the 2016 American presidential elections. Examples of information disseminated by individuals after accessing websites that informed them of the same included claims that well-known figures supported particular candidates. The assertions would later be revealed to the users to be false (Allcott & Gentzkow, 2017). The intended effect would have already taken place by that point, and it is suggested that such incidents may have contributed to determining how the elections turned out.

Social Media and Society

Social media offers a setting where people can share personal, group, or cultural interests and form connections with those who share their opinions and values or hold different ones. For instance, because they grew up in the same time period, most people in a specific age group have parallel concerns (Olanet et al. (2022). People frequently inherit their traits from their families, communities, and places of study. Further, as evidenced by the public's reactions to the 2016 and 2020 U.S. presidential elections as well as the 2019 U.K. general election, particular age categories continue to hold on to particular morals and ideas light of this, Venkatraman et al. (2018) stated that morals and views are transmitted across family generations, enabling a societal group to maintain particular ideologies.

Baur et al. (2020) indicated that, in social media is crucial in assisting people to maintain relationships with their friends and relatives, obtain employment, and make purchases of goods and services. A long-held worldview can be continued and spread by enlisting interested parties through social media platforms. Additionally, Baur et al. (2020) indicated that those that have similar demographic characteristics communicate more through instant messaging on S.M. than those who do not. Therefore, social media platforms are online services replicating activities in the real world.

The policy of societal acceptability can prevent the spread of fake news on social media (Sommariva et al., 2018). Nevertheless, the proliferation of numerous contact platforms for content and information distribution on social media platforms really has a more significant negative influence on the propagation of false information than positive ones. However, public acceptance is believed to fundamentally alter how fake news via social media is propagated (Egelhofer & Lecheler, 2019). Few empirical studies have looked at how fake news spreads and circulates online (Olan et al., 2022); Gray et al. (2020).), and even fewer have looked at how social decision can tell the truth from falsehood. Understanding the triangle of fake news the connections between the ideas from every circle, and the ties that unite the circles are crucial for reducing the transmission of fake news in society. Next, one should assess how strong each connection is.

Consequently, social media has a framework that serves as an environment for fake news flowing (Conroy et al., 2015). The social media structure hopes to create content that receives multiple perception through information or news delivery across targeted group of viewers. According to Mettler & Winter (2016), social media organizations are targeting higher profits as the components become popular and go viral in society. Considerably, social media structure is built primarily on a contents ranking system created using algorithmic ranking techniques, a data administration approach, and implication steamrolling in data significance (Hamamreh & Awad, 2017). The latest information is ranked according to a methodology that connects social media nodes to create a natural distribution.

By generating an iterative procedure of content in the network and assigning these weights in accordance with the content structure of each social media node, a unique code is created for each node in order to understand the ranking system (Brennen, 2017).. The surroundings for contagious content like fake news according to consist of channels of communication like websites, mobile apps, and systems that facilitate the development of relationships between users of content with similar interests (Hamamreh & Awad, 2017). From this perspective, the applicability of social media to diverse life aspects is highly significant to users, public policy, and the economic states.

Malicious social media accounts that spread misinformation Possibly Egelhofer & Lecheler, (2019) indicated that while there are many respectable social media users, some of them can be harmful or even not actual people. Given the low cost of opening a social media account, harmful users like trolls, cyborg clients, and social bots are also encouraged to open accounts. A social media platform run by a computer procedure known as a "social bot" automatically creates material and engages in social media interactions with users who are human or other bots. Social media manipulation and the broadcasting of false information on social media are only two examples of how social bots can turn into hostile entities with the intent to cause harm. According to Allcott & Gentzkow (2017), social media bots significantly influenced the 2016 U.S. presidential election online conversations and in the previous week prior to the elections, almost 19 million bot accounts indicated Trump of Clinton support through tweets.

Considerably, trolls, who are actual people using the internet to disrupt online communities and elicit emotional reactions from users are also popular in disseminating false information on social media. For instance, according to the evidence by Aro (2016), there may have been 1,000 paid Russian trolls distributing false information on Hillary Clinton. The environment of online talks and people's moods significantly impact trolling habits, making it simple to spread false information inside otherwise "regular" online communities. Trolling incites people's repressed negative thoughts, such as wrath and fear, which leads to mistrust and irrational conduct. Finally, individuals that combine automated processes with human input might spread false information. Typically, cyborg platforms are generated by people to operate in isolation through automation and then set up to carry out tasks on social media. According to Shu et al. (2017), cyborg users have a unique opportunity to distribute false information thanks to the simple transition between human and bot functionalities. In a word, these political, extremely active, and malevolent accounts on social media serve as significant sources for the spread of false information.

Methodology

The study deployed a qualitative research method to determine how new social media impacts the media platform. The issue of fake news in different social perspectives for new social media is critical and previous research on the issue depicts this. Through the qualitative technique, it was possible to understand the deep insights about the issue as it affects individuals and communities based on how they use the various social media platforms (Oun, & Bach, 2014). As such, a substantive literature review was deployed to gather the various insights from the selected sources. A substantive literature review is a sophisticated research technique that guides towards developing powerful insights that inform readers on the various issues associated with the given area explored. The standard features of the articles used were the underlying aspects that directed the research. The organization allowed for proper matching of the issues explored in the study.

Research Design

This study adopted an exploratory research design to determine how fake news is spread through social media platforms as they continuously gain popularity among users (Ponelis, 2015). The issue is that this research concept has been ignored, and most studies concentrate on social media as part of the technological development initiative that provides an opportunity for everyone to be engaged. Again, it has not been clear about the intensity in which have to suffer when they are extremely influenced by social media flames and related aspects connected to fake news. To develop robust findings in this research, previous studies were scrutinized in a manner that led to the establishment of different concepts that were then discussed deeply.

Search Criteria

To ensure that data was collected according to the targeted outcomes, criteria were used to align the various themes of the study. Peer-reviewed academic articles were found using the Discover Database for the study. This framework includes a variety of subject-related material types. It was essential to assess which papers were the most reliable and could produce a substantial and extensive literature review on this problem. The decision to use a specific database was also made with the knowledge that the research topic would be thoroughly investigated.

One goal of gathering information from secondary sources is to gain specific insights. As such, keywords and phrases were used to drive this effect. "Fake news," "New social media news biases," "Social media fake news," and "Social media frames." These phrases guided on the best articles to pick for the research. These terms guided towards generating 150 articles which was a relatively smaller number than using the general terms.

In order to narrow the search and guarantee that more precise materials were found, Boolean operators were used. In this study, "AND" "OR," and "NOT" were utilized. These operators' primary use was to include and exclude terms (Pazhaniraja et al., 2020). Their use was crucial since some of the undesirable items could be simply removed, leaving only the more important articles based on the research area. Additionally, it appeared that not enough research had been done on how to care for elderly dementia patients, making it challenging to find the precise information one would deem absolutely necessary. If employed for this research, the Boolean operators also saved time by eliminating text that seemed out of focus and increased errors. After using these, just 32 articles remained because the others appeared not to meet the requirements.

Findings

The purpose of this research was to examine how fake news affected society and how social media was used as a podium for the dissemination of news and information. As a result of this, Lazer et al. (2018) depicted that model of the disease triangle, which identifies fake news as an opportunistic problem in the absence of social acceptability, is further explored in this work. Furthermore, according to the definition used in this study, fake news has three key characteristics that are important for how society perceives it: the news's intentions, its content, and its veracity. Therefore, using a comparative technique to summarize the results of this study suggests that it's crucial to comprehend how fake affects society.

This study constructed a literature search aspect and examined the interactions between the characteristics of the three constructs inside it to comprehend better fake news, social media, and societal acceptance. To evaluate the issue, the information gathered from the qualitative literature review was additionally characterized as the associations intended in the paradigms. Through the lens of content management, this study examined social media platforms and the behaviors that encourage fake news spiraling processes, shift public acceptance and misinformation.

Social media platforms have been evaluated as the ecosystem for business and social exchanges with a focus on acquiring huge following for data delivery, which has furthered the spread of fake news through the application of the delivery tools, according to previous studies explored in this intervention. These studies have shown that social media platforms are transforming the business practices and techniques especially in product positioning and claim that cascading of fake news via social media platforms is expanding more quickly than expected. The findings of this study pointed to specific places where fake news on social media can be contained.

The findings from the data analysis showed significant contributions from this study to reducing the spread of false information in society. By taking into account the entities from each perspective, the relationship mapping was further refined by the evaluation of the perspectives of fake news impact and social acceptance.

Fake News Impact

The dangers of fake news spread through new social media cannot be ignored, as the literature findings indicated. It has been used to sway politics and advance commercial interests by using social media platforms to deliberately and demonstrably spread false information. New social media has also evolved into a strategy for igniting and escalating social conflict. Growing mistrust among Americans is a result of stories that are false and purposefully mislead readers. Sometimes, this suspicion leads to rudeness, protests over made-up tragedies, or even violence. This tears apart the social fabric of American society and pits neighbors against one another. Who would do this for a reason? Individuals, groups, and governments use false news for two distinct purposes, including those of foreign countries and even our own. In order to erode people's confidence in democracy and their capacity for cooperation, they start by escalating social conflict (Han et al., 2017). Then, they divert attention away from pressing concerns, causing them to remain unresolved. The use of fake news to divert attention and escalate conflict is examined in this section.

In one notable instance, as discussed in this research, a fake news item inspired one male suspect to open fire on a pizzeria that was linked to human smuggling and a presidential candidate because of misleading assertions. In the

"Pizzagate" event, a man approached Comet Ping Pong, a standard pizza outlet in Washington, DC, with a semi-automatic rifle, and started shooting. He was certain that a covert human trafficking network was being conducted out of the eatery by Hillary Clinton and her presidential race. This false narrative was first created by alt-right organizations, and it was promoted by fake news websites by making references to particular areas, including Comet Ping Pong. After being tweeted by individuals in the Czech Republic, Cyprus, and Vietnam as well as countless bots, the story gained even more attention (Gaozhao, 2021). Politically motivated fake news led a guy to open fire inside this restaurant, almost murdering diners. Spreading intentionally misleading information could have terrible repercussions especially when a sensitive issue if involved. This has always prevailed in the American society which is an epicenter of the world information delivery ideas.

Fake news can be used maliciously to escalate the national dispute in the US. Foreign authorities, like the Russian Internet Research Agency, American administrative strategists who deployed improperly acquired Facebook statistics from an established firm to influence social media clients voting decisions, as well as politically driven organizations, like the alt-right and alt-left, , were among the many bases of politically driven false information. They spread similar false information despite having different objectives.

The desire of SM enterprises to grow the volume of big data, which results in the deliberate end-to-end node multiplication, is responsible for the rise in the amount of fake news cascades. This analysis shows that SM company structure and practices are responsible for the favorable climate that allowed fake news to spread. The traffic of fake news is reduced, as is the impact on society when SM businesses put good fact-checking tools on social media platforms. The relevant function of SM firms is to ensure that gathering news and data includes validation and fact-checking.

Societal Acceptance

Concepts on technology acceptance explain what aspects of technology make it more or less probable to be adopted in a community or society. It investigates elements including users' attitudes about technology and the impact of technology's utility on acceptance. The technology acceptance literature has already been looked into in a number of contexts, including places of work consumer and online social networking sites However, these investigations have not been done in the context of fake news dissemination.

Studies have also examined electronic word-of-mouth literature, such as message comprehensibility and consumer propensity to accept different word-of-mouth messages. The word-of-mouth perspective advantage in relation to this study is that it concentrates on communications that have similarities to the news or fake news that was the subject of this investigation. However, although emphasizing technology above messaging, the literature on technology adoption adds value by providing methods to assess and gauge acceptance and use.

First off, the majority of everyday media consumption is unrelated to the news. Young adults consume news for much reduced time compared to the previous groups and in general, but across all age categories, non-news spending outweighs news intake. News is outpaced by a number of other subcategories for online consumption, which cover mobile and computer, such as recreation, social media, and searches. As depicted from the study by Aldwairi & Alwahedi, A. (2018), only a small proportion of all internet consumption is made up of the news, even when taking into account inactive contact to news materials on social media platforms like.

Despite the reduced instance of social media presenting news, the little presented in terms of fake news is what forms the critical problem in society. The general perspective is that a small issue in social media escalates into a significant issue considering that the social media platforms are continuously increasing the number of users at any time. A critical issue is that people readily accept what is presented to them without determining the authority of the source. The freedom that has developed in using social media, especially in modern society, is overwhelming.

It appears that all generations have accepted social media as an expression platform and a place where they can present information without many repercussions on them. The way in which people can also hide identity by using robotic mechanisms is also a significant problem that has led to the use of technology in the new social media as a privilege. The cutting edge is the situation where easy access to gadgets such as smartphones that provide personal internet connection becomes highly pronounced.

Consequently, an issue leading to increased acceptability of fake news on new social media is the poor analytical skills among the affected groups. Considering that people cannot wait to have the actual evidence on the issue, there is a high probability of rushing matters only for people to realize that they sometimes trust fake news when it is too late. Then, the emerging technologies allow people to adjust information through formatting so that the end user receives formatted information rather than what was originally acquired (Monsees, 2020). The intensity in which the fake news spread raises the primary question of how information can be trusted considering its content.

Misinformation

Misinformation refers to spreading information without the intent to cause harm. However, those spreading this news only realize to have done wrong when it is too late, and the issue cannot be reversed. This study identified that fake news is usually a probability of causing chaos by spreading wrong information to the audience (Chiluwa, & Samoilenko, 2019). Misinformation leads those receiving the information to react to the information in a manner that sometimes destroys their reputation or that of others who received the details.

The concept that fake news spreads faster than true news is considerable based on its impact. The exaggerations in this news are some of the reasons making them popular among social media users. Users also tend to increase the sharing of fake news at a high intensity, and the comments they associate with are also highly influential. There is much disorder caused, and when the necessary care is not taken, there is an increased probability of more problems caused than what is expected. In addition to allowing fragmentation, the widespread use of socially available technical platforms and micro-blogging outlets on the World Wide Web has altered how people are informed, engage in discourse, and develop opinions.

This unmediated environment may lead to misunderstandings about the cause of an event, which could lead to rumors, speculative behavior, and distrust. A blogger stated in 2011 that global warming was a hoax intended to restrict liberty and undermine democracy. Healthcare professionals have been confused by false information regarding the Ebola pandemic. An uncomplicated military drill called Jade Helm 15 was misinterpreted online as the start of a new civil war in the United States. The underlying anonymity and freedom of expression are escalating misinformation beyond measure.

According to Rodríguez et al. (2020) the World Economic Forum (WEF) has identified widespread digital disinformation as one of the major challenges to our society as it spreads over online social media. Algorithm-driven approaches have been put forth to buck this trend. For instance, Google is creating a trustworthiness score to prioritize search results. Facebook has also suggested a community-driven strategy in which users can report bogus information to change the newsfeed algorithm. However, this topic is contentious since it raises concerns that the proposed algorithms may not be precise or effective and that the free flow of content may be jeopardized. Conspiracy theorists frequently accuse those who try to refute incorrect information of spreading misinformation.

Conclusion

Fake news and clickbait make it difficult for social media users to distinguish between reputable information from Internet services, especially when the details are essential for making decisions. Fake news has grown to be more than just a marketing concern in the modern business environment, necessitating substantial efforts from security researchers. Any attempts to use fake news or clickbait to manipulate or troll the Internet must be stopped immediately and effectively. We suggested a straightforward yet efficient method for consumers to install a straightforward program into their individual site and use it to find and filter out possible clickbait. This essay is an initial attempt to offer a thorough and critical analysis of the subject of false news. In order to research fake news and its effects on consumer behavior, previous studies have generally chosen a more empirical scientific approach, such as trials. Our current understanding of fake news is advanced in three ways by a systematic review methodology. It identifies three things: 1) a wide range of academic disciplines that have studied fake news; the distinctive traits or features that false information has that can be used to help consumers detect it; and 3) a group of themes that summarize the issues that have been discussed and their interconnections, summarized through the proposed framework. Social standards and a claim's consistency with the person's belief system, or confirmation bias, significantly impact whether an individual accepts it. A variety of processes spreads false news, and once false beliefs are formed, they are seldom changed.

References

Aldwairi, M., & Alwahedi, A. (2018). Detecting fake news in social media networks. Procedia Computer Science, 141, 215-222.

Allcott, H., & Gentzkow, M. (2017). Social media and fake news in the 2016 election. Journal of economic perspectives, 31(2), 211-36.

Allcott, H., Braghieri, L., Eichmeyer, S., & Gentzkow, M. (2020). The welfare effects of social media. American Economic Review, 110(3), 629-76.

Aro, J. (2016). The cyberspace war: propaganda and trolling as warfare tools. European view, 15(1), 121-132.

Baur, N., Graeff, P., Braunisch, L., & Schweia, M. (2020). The quality of big data. Development, problems, and possibilities of use of process-generated data in the digital age. Historical Social Research/Historische Sozialforschung, 45(3), 209-243.

Brennen, B. (2017). Making sense of lies, deceptive propaganda, and fake news. Journal of Media Ethics, 32(3), 179-181.

Burkhardt, A. (2010). Social media: A guide for college and university libraries. College & research libraries news, 71(1), 10-24.

Carr, C. T., & Hayes, R. A. (2015). Social media: Defining, developing, and divining. Atlantic journal of communication, 23(1), 46-65.

Chen, Z. F., & Cheng, Y. (2019). Consumer response to fake news about brands on social media: the effects of self-efficacy, media trust, and persuasion knowledge on brand trust. Journal of Product & Brand Management.

Chiluwa, I. E., & Samoilenko, S. A. (Eds.). (2019). Handbook of research on deception, fake news, and misinformation online. IGI Global.

Conroy, N. K., Rubin, V. L., & Chen, Y. (2015). Automatic deception detection: Methods for finding fake news. Proceedings of the association for information science and technology, 52(1), 1-4.

Egelhofer, J. L., & Lecheler, S. (2019). Fake news as a two-dimensional phenomenon: A framework and research agenda. Annals of the International Communication Association, 43(2), 97-116.

Gaozhao, D. (2021). Flagging fake news on social media: An experimental study of media consumers' identification of fake news. Government Information

Quarterly, 38(3), 101591.

Gray, J., Bounegru, L., & Venturini, T. (2020). 'Fake news' as infrastructural uncanny. New media & society, 22(2), 317-341.

Hamamreh, R. A., & Awad, S. (2017, December). Tag Ranking Multi-Agent Semantic Social Networks. In 2017 International Conference on Computational Science and Computational Intelligence (CSCI) (pp. 899-903). IEEE.

Han, M., Yan, M., Cai, Z., Li, Y., Cai, X., & Yu, J. (2017). Influence maximization by probing partial communities in dynamic online social networks. Transactions on Emerging Telecommunications Technologies, 28(4), e3054.

Kim, J. H., Jung, S. H., Ahn, J. C., Kim, B. S., & Choi, H. J. (2020). Social networking sites self-image antecedents of social networking site addiction. Journal of Psychology in Africa, 30(3), 243-248.

Lazer, D. M., Baum, M. A., Benkler, Y., Berinsky, A. J., Greenhill, K. M., Menczer, F., ... & Zittrain, J. L. (2018). The science of fake news. Science, 359(6380), 1094-1096.

Mettler, T., & Winter, R. (2016). Are business users social? A design experiment exploring information sharing in enterprise social systems. Journal of Information Technology, 31(2), 101-114.

Mishra, A., & Samu, S. (2021). Impact of fake news on social image perceptions and consumers' behavioral intentions. Journal of Consumer Marketing.

Monsees, L. (2020). 'A war against truth'-understanding the fake news controversy. Critical Studies on Security, 8(2), 116-129.

Olan, F., Jayawickrama, U., Arakpogun, E. O., Suklan, J., & Liu, S. (2022). Fake news on social media: the Impact on Society. Information Systems Frontiers, 1-16.

Oun, M. A., & Bach, C. (2014). Qualitative research method summary. Qualitative Research, 1(5), 252-258.

Parry, E., & Solidoro, A. (2013). Social media as a mechanism for engagement?. In Social media in human resources management. Emerald Group Publishing Limited.

Pazhaniraja, N., Sountharrajan, S., & Sathis Kumar, B. (2020). High utility itemset mining: a Boolean operators-based modified grey wolf optimization algorithm. Soft Computing, 24(21), 16691-16704.

Ponelis, S. R. (2015). Using interpretive qualitative case studies for exploratory research in doctoral studies: A case of information systems research in small and medium enterprises. International Journal of Doctoral Studies, 10, 535.

Rodríguez, C. P., Carballido, B. V., Redondo-Sama, G., Guo, M., Ramis, M., & Flecha, R. (2020). False news around COVID-19 circulated less on Sina Weibo than on Twitter. How to overcome false information? International and Multidisciplinary Journal of Social Sciences, 9(2), 107-128.

Shu, K., Sliva, A., Wang, S., Tang, J., & Liu, H. (2017). Fake news detection on social media: A data mining perspective. ACM SIGKDD explorations newsletter, 19(1), 22-36.

Sommariva, S., Vamos, C., Mantzarlis, A., Đào, L. U. L., & Martinez Tyson, D. (2018). Spreading the (fake) news: exploring health messages on social media and the implications for health professionals using a case study. American journal of health education, 49(4), 246-255.

Venkatraman, S., & Alazab, M. (2018). Use of data visualisation for zero-day malware detection. Security and Communication Networks, 2018.

Von Jarelle, D. B., Peralta, K. M., Relucio, R. M. M., & Etrata Jr, A. E. Social Media Literacy and Misinformation: The Significance of Consuming Reliable Information in Relation to Shopper Buying Behavio

Contact information

Name of the author: Nnenna Uboma

Affiliation (University): LIGS University student

Email: nnenna.uboma@yahoo.ca

Fake News and New Social Media: Ghana's Legal Response

Dennis Owusu-Appiah Ofosuapea

Abstract

The world of media has moved on from the control of the media space by a selected few with the requisite training and responsibility to the control by all men and women in the world. This phenomenon has been liberated via the weapon of social media consequent to socialization of internet. When the authorities in the industry of fake news and social media posit that social media is a double-edged sword they mean that there is huge benefit of social media with its nefarious consequential orders of bad nuts. In Ghana like many other civilized nations, the men and women who control this social media space are equally controlled by the tenets of Constitution and the laws in the land. This article has discussed the phenomenon of fake news and new social media in Ghana, demonstrated the parameters of the Constitution and relevant related legal and statutory regimes with few case laws in the stated space. The evidence that emerged out of the discussed laws as stated, is that in Ghana fake news is criminalized notwithstanding the constitutional order of guaranteed rights of freedom of the media, speech, conscience and belief.

Keywords: *constitutional order, criminalized fake news, freedom of speech, guaranteed rights, social media.*

JEL Classification: *K42, I25, I15, L82*

Introduction

Social media is a global phenomenon and this is an understatement.[7] The 4th industrial revolution is equally live in Ghana, at least with respect to these social media users. News on social media space is periodically generated by 8.8 million Ghanaians as at August, 2022.[9] This number constitutes 29.33% of the 30.8 million Ghanaians as per the consensus numbers of the Ghanaian population.[12] The numbers have increased from a little over 4.6 million as at 2017 to the 8.8 million as at January, 2022. A projection thus can logically be gleaned as 300% in the next five years. Fake news generated in the social media space by a just a fraction of these stated users could pose a nightmare security concerns for the managers of the Country Ghana. Consequently, over the last 12 years the National Security with her detailed actors has been on the alert and intelligence in the stated space has heightened with a swift and merciless response to the skin of perpetrators.

Ghana has provided in the highest law in the land expressing the sovereign will of the people, [3] the 1992 Constitution, a guaranteed right of freedom of speech and expression of which constitutional rights include freedom of the press and the media. [10] This paper thus will review the scope of this legal regime within the meaning of the constraint justified by the Constitution on the stated rights. The ultimate aim is to establish the Ghana legal response to the menace of fake news in the space of social media.

The issue of social media & related matters

Social media as the name itself posits, is a media driving and run by the society, even though it has forcefully ben argued that no such definition could easily be had theoretically and functionally. [8] It is nonetheless an extension of the right to express ones belief, opinion, conscience and thoughts for as Harry H. Wellington stated in his article: **On Freedom of Expression 88 Yale LJ 1105**;[26] the learned author concluded that the free speech is the nerve of all other basic rights. No wonder the intellectual colossal John Stuart Mill, in his **On Liberty (1859) Ch. 2**, [18] immortally posited the significance of the concept thus: "If all mankind minus one were of one opinion, mankind would be no more justified in silencing that one person than he, if he had the power, would be justified in silencing mankind."[6][22]

In today's world, there is a mounting number of medium through which the society does her business of living anchored by their respective belief, opinion, conscience and thought. These include: Facebook, YouTube, WhatsApp, Instagram, Twitter, WeChat, TikTok, & LinkedIn, inter alia.

Collectively this medium holds over 4.8 billion human beings out of the near 8 billion souls on the planet earth, constituting near 58.4% of the global population.[15] In short, suggestively, social media is comparable to more than 50% of world physical surface occupation: everybody is there operating or watching or both.

Consequently, these mediums offer the society a forum to exercise their right of free speech, socialization, political engagement, marketing of their trade and wears, and even the force of military warfare,[16] inter alia. To restrict it in any form and or substance therefore must be justified by law and compromise for United Nations has declared it a universal basic right and it shall be so for a long time to come.[13]

The concept of fake news

It has been firmly reported that fake news is historical in nature and form and as far back as 1857 India gossip that landed the country in what had become Sepoy Mutiny land greased issue with a nationwide spectacle, is quite an example. The difference today is the currency of seconds carried by the internet on the social media space.

Fake news is thus a falsehood machine powered by a velocity of reaching dozens of social media users via the internet in the social media space.[4] It takes the form of voice, writings, photos and videos and or even coded language, inter alia, to do its damage.

Fake news is often planed, well-resourced and effectively executed and it has been suggested fake news go beyond false news.[20] The result is that, it often achieves its mission and confused the system and its targeted audience.[17]

Global response to fake news

It is logistical nightmare to effectively monitor a periodic "12½ trillion hours spent online...." by the citizens of the world, a finding reported by Digital 2022. Nonetheless, due to the reckless and diabolic nature of fake news, the world has quickly responded to its effect by counterbalancing its outcomes.[14] The actors in the counterbalancing block have been supra-nations such as the European Union as well as individual nations such as Ghana, Qatar and Singapore.

The global response takes the form of laws, policies, regulations and institutions specifically set up to deal with the ills of the fake news menace.[25] As Vasu et al (2018) report as finding, these supra-nations and or nations have set up websites for example to deal with the menace: "... Europe, Stopfake.org...2014 to combat ...fake news ...during Ukraine's crises in Crimea."; "... Qatar, Lift the Blockade... in 2017..." fake news which sought to justify economic blockade on Qatar by her geopolitical rivals; and "... Singapore, Factually..." was to combat misrepresentation and misinformation on Government policy.[25]

Ghana response to fake news

In order to appreciate the Ghanaian response to the fake news menace, it is important to understand the legal regime within the meaning of the constitutional order within which the rights of freedom of speech and expression are guaranteed.[5]

It is thus provided under article 21 (1) (a) of the Constitution 1992 thus: "All persons shall have the right to freedom of speech and expression, which shall include freedom of the press and other media."

The right to free speech under this law includes other media of which other media includes social media. The rights issues under the stated law have found expression in number of domestic cases. Few of these cases shall be discussed hereunder to bring to life the scope and meaning of the stated law on the subject under reference.

NEW PATRIOTIC PARTY v. GHANA BROADCASTING CORPORATION [1993-94]2 GLR 354[21]

Plaintiff, one of the leading political parties in Ghana, sued the Defendant, the main state broadcaster, TV and Radio, for free speech by way of equal air space for their political programs for both presidential and parliamentary elections in the Republic of Ghana.

In declaring the rights sought for by the Plaintiff as constitutionally guaranteed rights, the Supreme Court of the Republic of Ghana held, inter alia, thus: fair opportunity ought to be given to all to present their programs to the public and this ought to be in the form of equal access to the state owned media. The term equal access meant entry ought to be based on the same terms and conditions meeting of them entitled one to enjoy equal space. The word fair was interpreted to mean no bias and or prejudice. The only limitation was stated to include well-defined laws with stated grounds of national interest by way of national security, public order, and public morality and for the protection of other people's rights of reputation and freedoms.

REPUBLIC v. INDEPENDENT MEDIA CORPORATION OF GHANA & ORS [1996-97] SCLR 258[24]

The Republic of Ghana charged the accused persons in this Matter for the offence of unauthorized use of radio frequency contrary to section 15(b) of the Telecommunications (Frequency and Registration and Control) Act, 1997. Under the stated law one could not use a radio frequency in Ghana without first seeking and acquiring a written consent of the Board under the stated law and accused person violated the stated provision as charged. Before Circuit, Accra, the Accused raised preliminary legal objection as to the constitutionality of the impugned section. The objection was accordingly referred to the Supreme Court by the sitting judge in compliance of the Ghanaian constitutional order.

It was held that the stated section was not unconstitutional as the restrictions and impediments imposed by the licensing regime were necessary for the protection of national security, public order, and public morality and for further protection of the reputations of others and their respective legal rights.

GHANA INDEPENDENT BROADCASTERS ASSOCIATION (No. 2) v. ATTORNEY GENERAL & NATIONAL MEDIA COMMISSION (No. 2) [2017-2020] SCGLR 505[11]

Plaintiff, an association of media houses in Ghana, sued the Defendants, state institutions and or officials, for a declaration that requirement for content authorization and the procedure in securing this content authorization under the National Media Commission (Content Standards) Regulations, 2015 (LI 2224), are unconstitutional and thus void and of no legal effect.

The Supreme Court held that the impugned regulations under LI 2224 are unconstitutional and thus void *ab initio* for a legislation that imposes such restriction to be constitutional it ought to meet the test of protection of national security, public order, and public morality and for further protection of the reputations of others and their respective legal rights. Those regulations stated failed the stated constitutional test.

The Court further held that other significant part of the LI 2224 such as those that define proper criminal sanctions by way of punishment for exercise of media freedom is a limit that is justified under the constitution and same is a constitutional function conferred on the 2nd Defendant. The court cannot strike down a penal legislation because the various forms of punishment prescribed therein are too harsh, the court further held.

Penal Code & Related Matters

Publication of false news is proscribed and criminalized in the Republic of Ghana. under the law, the position is stated thus: " A person who publishes or reproduces a statement of, rumour or report which is likely to cause fear and alarm to the public or to disturb the public peace, knowingly or having reason to believe that the statement , rumour or report is false commits a misdemeanor."[1]

It is further provided under subsection 2 of section 208 of Act 29, as amended, thus: that no defence lies to the protection of a suspect and or accused under the stated law above that he or she was unaware that the impugned report, rumour or statement was false. The only ground capable of credible defence is that the accused person before publication of the false news engaged in credible verification to authentic the accuracy of the impugned report, rumour or statement.

ADUSEI II v. THE REPUBLIC [1975]2 GLR 225[2]

The Appellant in this case sent a letter to a sitting Asantehene claiming certain persons had hashed a plan to stage coup d'etat in Ghana and upon investigation by the police there was no evidence of such a plan. The Accused was accordingly charged for publishing false news, tried, convicted and sentenced.

Upon an appeal to the High Court, it was held that the offence was not proved. The appeal was allowed and the reason was thus stated: for the stated offence to be made, publication alone is not enough but it is necessary to prove that the said report, rumour, and or statement is likely to go against public tranquility. The Republic failed to sufficiently establish the likely end result of disorder in public place and thus conviction and sentence was accordingly reversed and Accused set free, acquitted and discharged.

REPUBLIC v. AMINA MUHAMMED (A.K.A AMINA YUTONG BUS), unreported.[19][23]

The accused person, a 24 year Ghanaian woman, was charged under section 208 of Act 29 for falsely publishing that as a passenger on a Yutong Bus, she witnessed a mass armed robbery and rape on the stated bus and the rape included her own 14 year old daughter.

The High Court, Accra, held that the Republic had failed to make a prima facie case against the Accused capable of sustaining calling upon the Defendant to open her defence. The Matter was thus struck out. The Court reasoned that there was no credible evidence that any alarm and or public order was disturbed and or at all.

Conclusion

In Ghana like many other civilized nations, the men and women who control this social media space are equally controlled by the tenets of Constitution and the laws in the land. This article has discussed the phenomenon of fake news and new social media in Ghana, demonstrated the parameters of the Constitution and relevant related legal and statutory regimes with relevant case laws in the stated space. The evidence that emerged out of the discussed laws as stated is that in Ghana fake news is criminalized notwithstanding the constitutional order of guaranteed rights of freedom of the media, speech, conscience and belief.

It is however clear from the discussed cases that even though there is a potent legislation in place to deal adequately with the issue of fake news in Ghana, the Ghanaian courts are jealous vanguards of free speech as guaranteed and fundamental rights of the Ghanaian citizens. It is thus of high bar to establish the stated offence against a charged citizen. It appears that the courts are more interested in the likely effects than the cause of a stated publication. It may thus mean that necessary amendments are made to the existing legislation for a strict liability situation and or the Republic ought to rely on a more frugal policy in reaching compromise and or consensus in dealing with fake news menace as argued by Gillani, Ishfaq and ud Din in this field.

References

1. Acts of Ghana (n-d), Criminal and Other Offences Act (1960), Act 29, as amended section 208(1). https://www.ilo.org/dyn/natlex/docs/ELECTRONIC/88530/101255/F575989920/GHA88530.pdf

2. ADUSEI II v. THE REPUBLIC [1975]2 GLR 225

3. Atuguba R. (2020). The concept of sovereignty in Ghanaian constitutionalism, International Journal of Human Rights and Constitutional Studies 2020 Vol.7 No.1

4. Bajo C. (2019) Fake news and censorship in Africa, https://lab.cccb.org/en/fake-news-and-censorship-in-africa/

5. BIMPONG-BUTA S. (2017). THE ROLE OF THE SUPREME COURT IN THE DEVELOPMENT OF CONSTITUTIONAL LAW IN GHANA, https://uir.unisa.ac.za/bitstream/handle/10500/2386/thesis.pdf?isAllowed=y&sequence=1

6. Bujnoch L. (2019). Understanding Necessity in War and Conflict, https://theses.gla.ac.uk/81421/1/2019BujnochPhD.pdf

7. Butkowski C., Dixon T., & Weeks R. (2019). Quantifying the feminine self(ie):

Gender display and social media feedback in young women's Instagram selfies, https://doi.org/10.1177/1461444819871669

8. Carr C. & Hayes R. (2015). Social Media: Defining, Developing, and Divining, https://www.tandfonline.com/doi/abs/10.1080/15456870.2015.972282

9. Dokuah D. (2022), Total number of active social media users in Ghana from 2017 to 2022, https://www.statista.com/statistics/1171445/number-of-social-media-users-ghana/#:~:text=Number%20of%20active%20social%20media%20users%20in%20Ghana%202017%2D2022&text=As%20of%20January%202022%2C%20Ghana,million%20in%20the%20preceding%20year.

10. Faanu P. & Graham E. (2017). The Politics of Ethnocentrism: A Viability Test of Ghana's Democracy? https://doi.org/10.1177/0975087817715534

11. GHANA INDEPENDENT BROADCASTERS ASSOCIATION (No. 2) v. ATTORNEY GENERAL & NATIONAL MEDIA COMMISSION (No. 2) [2017-2020] SCGLR 505

12. Ghana Statistical Service (2021), 2021 Population and Housing Census, https://census2021.statsghana.gov.gh/

13. Gillani A, Ishfaq N. & ud Din M. (2021). FREEDOM OF EXPRESSION AS A BASIC HUMAN RIGHT IN PAKISTAN: A FANTASY OR A REALITY? https://55.+Vol,+3.+Issue+3.+Sept+2021+Gillani,+Ishfaq,+&+Zia+ud+Din+Freedom+of+Expression+as+a+Basic+Human+Right+in+Pakistan.pdf

14. Greg S. (2018). Fake News: As the Problem or a Symptom of a Deeper Problem? https://uu.diva-portal.org/smash/get/diva2:1181745/FULLTEXT01.pdf

15. Kemp S. (2022).Digital 2022: Global Overview Report: https://datareportal.com/reports/digital-2022-global-overview-report

16. Mayfield T. (2008). A Commander's Strategy for Social Media, https://indianstrategicknowledgeonline.com/web/mayfield_strat_for_soc_media.pdf

17. Mensah K, Awini G & Mensah G. (2021).Fake News and SDG1: The Situation in Ghana, The Palgrave Handbook of International Communication and Sustainable Development pp 325–344

18. Mill J. (1859), On Liberty Ch. 2.

19. Modern Ghana (2012). Yutong Bus Mass Rape Case: Court Sets Amina Free, https://www.modernghana.com/news/400657/yutong-bus-mass-rape-case-court-sets-amina-free.html

20. Mollina M, Sundar S. & Le T. (2019) “Fake News” Is Not Simply False Information: A Concept Explication and Taxonomy of Online Content, https://doi.org/10.1177/0002764219878224

21. NEW PATRIOTIC PARTY v. GHANA BROADCASTING CORPORATION [1993-94]2 GLR 354

22. Oxford University Press (2017), Oxford Essential Quotations, (5 edn). https://www.oxfordreference.com/view/10.1093/acref/9780191843730.001.0001/q-oro-ed5-00007298

23. REPUBLIC v. AMINA MUHAMMED (A.K.A AMINA YUTONG BUS), unreported.

24. REPUBLIC v. INDEPENDENT MEDIA CORPORATION OF GHANA & ORS [1996-97] SCLR 258

25. Vasu N. et al (2018).FAKE NEWS: NATIONAL SECURITY IN THE POST-TRUTH ERA,

https://www.jstor.org/stable/resrep17648.8?seq=1#metadata_info_tab_contents

26. Wellington H. (n-d.) On Freedom of Expression 88 Yale LJ 1105

Contact information

Name of the author: Dennis Owusu-Appiah Ofosuapea

Affiliation (University): LIGS University student

Email: ohenebahkwadwo@gmail.com

The Battle of Fake News in Social Media: Case of Political Elections in Indonesia

Richardus Eko Indrajit

Abstract

As a democratic country with a decentralized system, Indonesia implements a direct election system for its leaders and representatives of the people who sit in parliament. Every year there are more than 100 regional head election events. To win the election, the candidate and his team develop various ways and strategies. In modern times, the most widely used communication and campaign channel is social media. Besides being cheap, social media in developing countries such as Indonesia is considered very effective in its use. However, problems arise when the candidate winning team uses a notorious strategy to spread fake news to win. This article results from a study that aims to describe a winning strategy for utilizing fake news via social media over the last ten years. The methodology used in this research is the observation of various violations during the election because the candidate team spreads fake news that puts down opposing candidates or glorifies the candidates they propose. The study results show several modes of using fake news in social media wars during the election period.

Keywords: *Elections, Fake News, Social media media.*

JEL Classification: *Z13: Economic Sociology • Economic Anthropology • Language • Social and Economic Stratification*

Introduction

Since reforms were introduced in 1998, Indonesia has changed its government system from centralization to decentralization. One of the impacts of this change is the obligation of the people in each region to directly elect their respective regents or mayors. The candidate who gets the most votes from the public will be appointed as the region's leader. Considering that Indonesia has more than 500 regions, in one period of government (5 years), there are 500 regional head elections or approximately one hundred elections per year. Statistics show that more than 85% of regional election ends in a contestation between two potential leaders. When these two candidates fought, each winning team applied its marketing strategy. Social media is the favourite of the various campaign instruments used because it is considered cheap, fast, massive, and effective (Allen et al., 2020). In this constellation, various hoaxes and fake news began to spread on social media, which misled the public and vote holders (Anderson & Sulistyani, 2019).

Material and Methods

This researcher analyzed the regional head elections from 2014 to 2019. For six years, the researchers collected various data through campaign team posts on social media. The social media that became the basis of observation were Youtube, Facebook, Instagram, and Whatsapp. Table 1 shows the number of posts used as analysis material on the four related social media.

Table 1: Number of Posting Samples in Social Media

Year	Youtube	Facebook	Instagram	Whatsapp
2014	1,000	350	1,050	750
2015	1,000	360	1,120	770
2016	1,150	400	1,200	810
2017	1,250	420	2,100	880
2018	1,500	440	2,350	920
2019	2,000	520	2,770	975

Analysis was carried out on the post content of the campaign-winning teams to identify the communication patterns. Note that all selected posts have been validated as fake news or hoaxes. The method used is to use a data clustering approach.

Model and Data

The analysis was carried out on the campaign content in the regional head election of two candidate leaders. The results of data processing show several communication patterns as follows. First, the winning team simultaneously carried out dual strategies, namely by spreading false news that praised the candidate candidates and badmouthing the opposing party. Second, fake news content is distributed using a rational, emotional, and physical approach. Figure 1 shows a matrix constructed from these two dimensions.

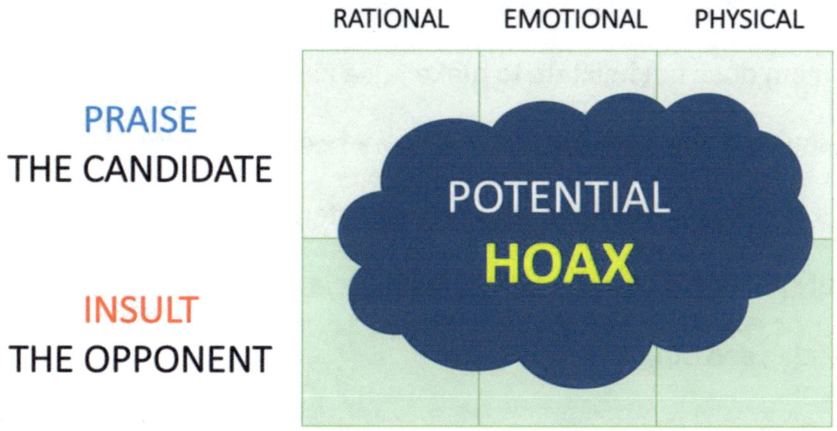

Figure 1: Two Dimensional Domain of Potential Hoax in the Election Events

Results and Discussion

Researchers conducted an in-depth analysis of the content of fake news that was spread. It can be seen that fake news with nuances of praising the winning candidates is narcissistic. The campaign team falsified their curriculum vitae, work performance, intellectual abilities, work performance, and personality profiles. Meanwhile, the way to vilify potential opponents is by spreading slanderous news through false stories. Even the winning team did not hesitate to make a hate speech against the opposing party. To create rational fake news content, they fabricate data, twist the logic of thinking, create a series of stories that look solid, fabricate information, and manipulate social media content (Howard et al., 2021;

Wang, 2020). Meanwhile, to cause an emotional effect among voters, the campaign team does not hesitate to make false news about candidates' past behaviour, expose disgrace that has never been done, spread false testimonies, and so on. The fake content that enters the physical domain is when identity politics is used by raising issues related to race, ethnicity, religion, gender, and others.

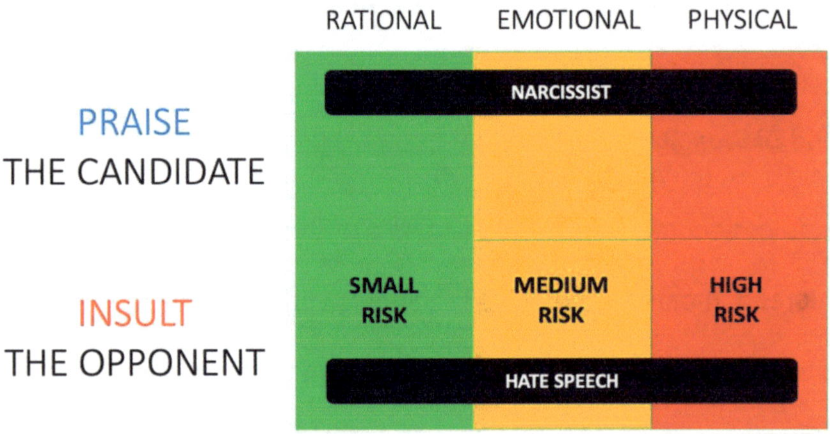

Figure 2: The Fake News Content and the Risk to Society

When the researchers connect hoaxes and fake news types with the resulting impact, it can be seen that there is an influence of different levels of risk (Verstraete et al., 2022).. Creating fake news that promotes identity politics is very dangerous because it is very sensitive (Pauli, 2018). A number of these fake news have proven to have caused several socio-cultural tensions in the community. Meanwhile, fake news that touches rational and emotional elements has a low and medium risk level. Figure 2 shows the mapping of all these relations.

The subsequent analysis focuses on the language used in creating and disseminating fake news. The winning team for the regional head election has a precise strategy for classifying the target content (Pennycook & Rand, n.d.). Social media posts with content nuances that contain rational news such as work success, originality of vision, the creativity of ideas, and performance improvement appear to be aimed at the educated upper class. However, fake news equipped with much-supporting data and information will be able to influence them. Meanwhile, the winning team targets the middle class for hoax content that can move a person's emotional side. The reason is that you are a middle class consisting of women and young people who are very dynamic and sensitive to the situation around them. The fake news content that is created contains policies that harm people, unethical candidate behaviour, unsympathetic personality characteristics, and so on. For the general public, the majority of whom have low educational backgrounds, the winning team presented hoaxes related to issues of gender, race, ethnicity, disability, religion, and other stereotypes. This approach is used because lower levels of society easily understand it (Serstevens et al., 2022). Figure 3 shows the segmentation of the target recipients of fake news.

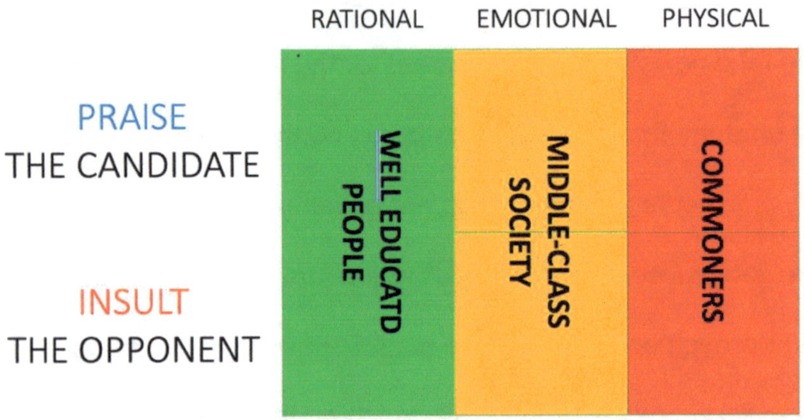

Figure 3: The Target Segment of Hoaxes and Fake News

All these notorious attempts were made to win the hearts of voters. They do not hesitate to create false narratives packaged to look authentic. Lots of dictions that flatter candidates and destroy the opponent's image are used as titles for social media posts. Table 2 shows several examples of perceptions people try to instil in people, so they decide to support one candidate and hate other candidates.

Table 2: Examples of Fake News Content in Various Dimension

Strategic Approach	Rational Fake News	Emotional Fake News	Physical Fake News
Praise the Candidate	• The candidate has succeeded in increasing the welfare of the people as long as he is a servant of the state. • The candidate has successfully completed his mission while serving as a community leader.	• The candidate is loved by the surrounding community because of his generosity • The candidate is a very friendly person and loves to help others • Candidates always sided with the poor and did not hesitate to act	• The candidate is a good and pious follower of the majority religion • Candidates come from ethnic groups that are highly valued • The candidate has absolutely no background related to illicit sects such as communism

	• The candidate is the initiator of a number of pro-community programs.	to fight injustice	
Insult the Opponent	• The opponent have never succeeded in implementing their programs while serving as a civil servant • The pponent always fail to meet the performance assigned to him while	• Opponents often show an unsympathetic attitude to the people around them • Opponents never pay attention to the plight of poor people who need state help • Opponents are often	• The opponent is a cult follower who endangers society • The opponent comes from a family of communist descent whose sects of understanding are prohibited by the state

	carrying out his duties as a leader • The opponent does not have sufficient background and experience to be trusted as a regional head	demonized by the public because of their arrogant, indifferent, and rude attitude	• The opponent comes from minority ethnic groups who do not have strong and solid state roots

Conclusion

The campaign-winning team uses fake news to increase its candidates' electability while destroying its opponent's credibility. This unsportsmanlike and unethical behaviour is carried out by utilizing social media. The fake news created is aimed respectively at the educated upper class, the dynamic middle class, and the ordinary people of diverse backgrounds.

Content that is used as fake news seeks to distort rationality, stir emotions, and inflame human physical instincts. The whole behaviour of spreading fake news presents no small risk because it can destroy the joints of social life. Therefore, people have to watch out for the existence of such fake news within society.

REFERENCES

References and bibliography

Allen, J., Howland, B., Mobius, M., Rothschild, D. & Watts, D. (2020). Evaluating the fake news problem at the scale of the information ecosystem. Science Advances Research Article.

Anderson, S. & Sulistyani, H.D. (2019). Detecting and combating fake news on web 2.0 technology in the 2019 political season Indonesia. Journal of Social Studies (JSS), Vol. 15. No. 2.

Howard, P.N., Neudert, L. & Prakash, N. (2021). Digital misinformation/disinformation and children. University of Oxford and UNICEF.

Pauli, C. (2018). "Fake News," No News, and the Needs of Local Communities. Texas A&M University School of Law.

Pennycook, G. & Rand, D.G. (n.d.). The Psychology of Fake News. Forthcoming in Trends in Cognitive Sciences.

Serstevens, F., Piccillo, G. & Grigoriev, A. (2022). Fake news zealots: Effect of perception of news on online sharing behavior. Frontiers in Psychology.

Verstraete, M., Bambauer, J.R. & Bambauer, D.E. (2022). Identifying and

Countering Fake News. Hasting Law Journal, Vol 73, Issue 3.

Wang, C. (2020). Fake News and Related Concepts: Definitions and Recent Research Development. Contemporary Management Research, Vol. 16, No. 3, Pages 145-174.

Contact information

Name of the author: Richardus Eko Indrajit

Affiliation: LIGS University (PhD Candidate)

Email: eko.indrajit@gmail.com

Fake News and the New Social Media: The perception of youth on implication and possible solution

Suwaiba Muhammad Dankabo

Abstract

According to researchers 1-10 twitter accounts is fake! (WGASTAFF 2013) Just like other new social media, twitter is one of the social platforms that presents an opportunity for social discuss and connecting people. In a world where information is power in which people rely on news as a means of social interaction and personal decision making, fake news present security threat to national unity and survival of individuals while exacerbating the menace of hate speech fueling social disruption. This paper analyses the implications of fake news in the new social media on the peace and security of a nation, with a focus on Nigeria. In writing this paper, 100 young people who are actively engaged on social media through Google Forms, using the 5ws&h analyses (what, why, who, where when, and how) on Fake News. Their responses along with desk review of well researched published papers on the same issue, presents possible solutions and alternative ventures for those engaged in the business of fake news in the new social media.

Keywords: *society, disruption, security, solution, alternative.*

JEL Classification: *Z130: Economic Sociology; Economic anthropology; language' Social and Economic Stratification.*

Introduction

Fake news is a statement of information that is not true, distorted information or wrongly processed data that is circulated with the aim of misinforming, sending a wrong signal, or influencing the thought process of a person or group of persons to make an opinion that favors the motive desired motive of the sender. The most common medium of passing fake news is the new social media. These includes but not limited to WhatsApp, Twitter, Facebook, etc.

Material and Methods

In the course of writing this paper, a survey was conducted through the

Google forms. 100 young people who are actively engaged in the social media were requested to use the 5Ws&H analyses and share opinions on Fake News and New Social Media, Out of 100 targeted, 45 persons responded to the questionnaire within two weeks of circulation in North - Eastern part of Nigeria. A follow up group discussion was conducted in FCT following discovery that some recipients of the google form suspected it to be a scam.

Defining Fake News: Participants understanding

Summarizing the opinion of participants of the survey, fake news is unverifiable information fabricated to mislead the general or targeted audience. It is a type of yellow journalism or propaganda, or hoaxes spread through the traditional or social media. Many categories of people are associated with the spread of fake news. It is believed that the new social media provides a comfortable zone for the activities of fake news actors. According to the participants of this survey, as presented on figure 2 below, politicians and youth top the list of those who spreads fake news, followed by unemployed and scammers. Others feel that anyone can spread fake news.

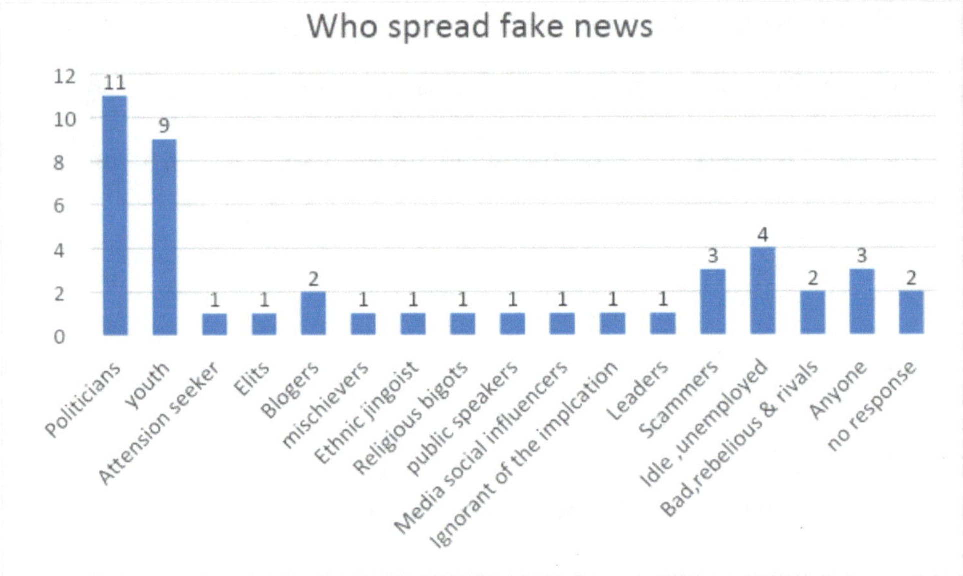

Figure 1 perception of participants on who spreads fake news

Why do people spread Fake News

In response to the reason why people spread fake news, participants identified 5 key categories of motives, vis political, image making for self-publicity, and defamation of other persons character. As illustrated on the table below.

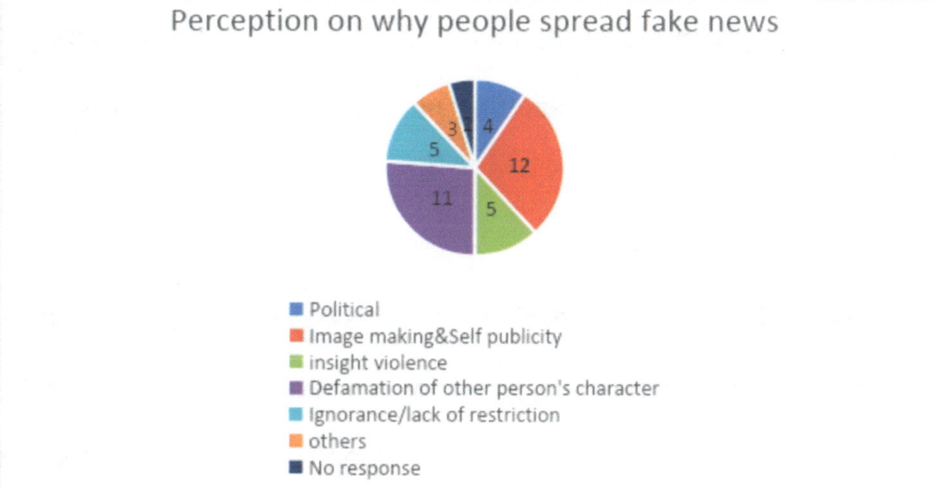

Figure 2 participant's perception on why people spread fake news

Tackling the menace of fake news in the new social media

Participants have recommended ways forward to curve the menace of fake news.

While recognizing the absence of restrictions on information posted on social media, the role of government in the regulation of social media through surveillance, filtering and blocking is strongly recommended. Participants also opined that fake news will be curtailed is perpetrators are trailed, apprehended, and prosecuted. On the part of the users of social media, participants suggest continued awareness creation through the same social media and religious outfits, as well as skills building on how to censor and verify information. Another control measure is for the owners of social media platforms, to secure the platforms through the application of relevant tools for flagging, reporting, and debugging unverified news.

Results and Discussion

Although Fake news dated back to centuries before the advent of the new social media, The internet plays a major role in facilitating the spread and consumption of harmful information as opined by the former WhatsApp vice-president Chris Daniels during an interview in 2018.

This study has revealed the role of politicians and Youth as major perpetrator of fake news. This is corroborated by Hidayat, who argued that politicians work through consultants < to craft> untrue stories in pursuit of their election prospect (Hidayat,2020, pp. 6) siting examples of how UK based media company collaborated with Israeli hackers to obtain and doctored information on a Nigerian political opponent during the 2015 elections.

There is no gainsaying that politicians take advantage of the youth and unemployed otherwise known as idle persons to use their space in perpetrating fake news in order to influence public opinion through the social media, in their favor. In doing so they explore various means of demeaning their opponents hate speech, character assassination etc. This action results in a vicious cycle, as oppositions and their supporters launch and sustains the tempo of revenge. The use of propaganda to create negative image of a siting government or hate speech among politicians and religious radicals is a common phenomenon in Nigeria, especially with availability of a free to access social media. Hence the unending conflicts among clans and political divide. These propagandas include biased disclosure of financial deals, fiscal allocations and public contract issues which attracts the attention of citizens on public resource allocation verses or justifications for the use of resources which are in contention. Figure3 presented in this report contains an information generated from Niger Republic but is used to portray achievement of Nigerian Army. This image created argument in the social media, WhatsApp to be precise, with the addition of just 2 letters, that changed Niger to Nigeria. Although the image portrays Nigerian Army's bravery, it encountered a backlash as citizens who are not happy with the level of accountability of fiscal resources allocated for counter terrorism. The argument went for a while and died down. No one knows the author.

The medium: New Social Media

Study conducted by CITAD, shows consistency of Facebook as a dominant means of dissemination of hate speech in Nigeria (CITAD,2019, pp. 2). This medium play host to 37 million Nigerians out of which 32.8% are aged youth aged between 25 to 34 years old (Dokua, 2022).

My page my space; the number of likes and followers determined the capacity of a person to catch a population's attention to an issue, the number of follower/friends/lokes is an attraction for marketing. In this space anything goes, the good, the bad and the ugly. Messages through the social media easily gets viral because of ease of access and opportunity for freedom to brand without restriction.

Mischievous people also spread fake news. The last decade feature more than 10 prominent fake obituaries of prominent people including celebrities, president religious leaders in Nigeria, for reason unknown. The pictures of prominent religious leaders in a heavily compromised positions floured over the media few months ago.

The implication of fake news in the new social media

Fake news is mostly spread during sensitive period; crises, war, or election period, the intention behind heating the polity on such occasions has been analyzed as a tool for escalation, diversion of public attention or interest from the main issue, facilitating corrupt practices, including diversion of public resources. This undermines the principle of good governance as the polity is built upon the pillars of deception, fake news set people against each other creates enmity and social divide, the factor responsible for unending violence, ethnic and religious conflict, and youth restiveness. Time spent in unhealthy discuss over social media deprives the nation of potential productive force whose energy can be channeled to rid the Country off poverty and exclusion. The phenomenon if not tackled will gradually erode democracy. Young people's talents used for creating and spreading fake news can be turned in to an effective means of critical mobilization and a meaningful venture through Concerted efforts of computer experts, sociologists, psychologists, government, and communities (Zapharani, R., et al. 2019)

Way forward

The technology is powerful, the business of fake news is lucrative, curving the menace is not an easy task collaborative effort between government and social media presents a ray of hope. Czech Republic implements a pilot scheme combining human expertise and technology. Behavioral change through conscientizing citizens on the features and impacts of fake news (Boagan, K. et-al, 2021) of digital entrepreneurship for young people with competitive advantage including legal patronage, linked with leadership and accountability.

Sanitizing the social media through regulation, proper identification, digital surveillance and tracking through effective collaboration between government and the social media to ensure charges and penalties for defaulters. Regulation of content on social media to include author's name, date, and location of event/incident or authentic signature without which news cannot pass or forwarded. Another strategy is to embrace holistic fight against corruption, supported by a reformed judiciary that will ensure timely prosecution of the corrupt. Accountable and transparent governance systems will free the society from the cravings for information on shabby dealings associated with corruption especially when accompanied by gender responsive public services and equitable distribution of resources.

Conclusion

The new social media has come to stay, its usage facilitates development of a nation in a positive or negative way. The last few decades have witnessed the proliferation of social media, through which people exchanges information flow, unfortunately a significant percentage of this information is confirmed to be fake. Unpatriotic Nigerians majority of whom are politicians and youth have spread fake news for ulterior motives, which has contributed to the stagnation of peace and security, while exacerbating a vicious cycle of political unrest, paving way for unending corruption and subsequently increasing poverty. The social media such as face book permeates fake news through which lucrative adverts find their ways. One critical example is the viral video of death toll in Kano State which appeared on face book two weeks after the incidence (CDD, 2020, pp.3) The energies of those perpetrating fake news can be channeled to positive ventures and the business of fake news can be controlled through regulation, enforcement, and prosecution.

Acknowledgements

This paper was written when during an intensive humanitarian response but was still possible through the support of CEO Center for Advocacy and Transparency Action Initiative, Borno, who helped in circulating Google forms to young people's platforms, Sunnyvale Sister Association FCT (WhatsApp group) made the FGDs very easy. LIGS University conference team were highly supportive being flexible and understanding of my condition.

References and bibliography

1. Boagan, K., Xiong, A. Lee, D., & Han, K. (2021). A systematic review on fake news research through the lens of news creation and consumption; Research efforts, challenges, and future directions. http://doi.org/10.1371/journal.pone.0260080
2. Hassan, H., Hitchen, J. (2020). Driving Division: Disinformation and the New Media Landscape
   in Nigeria
3. Jibrin, I., Ya'u, Y.Z. (2021). Context and Content in Hate Speech: Discourse in Nigeria
4. Ya'u, Y.Z. (2019). Politicians, Fake fakebook Profiles and the possibility of Being unwitting
   Hate Speech Purveyors
5. Zafari, R., Zhou, X., Shu, K. & Liu, H. (2019). Fake news research, theories, detection strategies, and open problems. KDD '19: proceedings of the 25th ACMSIGKDD international conference on knowledge discovery & data mining.
   https://doi.org/10.1145/3292500.3332287

Contact information

Name of the author: Suwaiba Muhammad Dankabo

Affiliation (University): LIGS University

Email: suwaibafirst2020@gmail.com

Healthcare text generated by AI has the potential to misinform and not be recognized as AI content by either healthcare professionals or the general public

Natalie Dubois Bourré, B.Sc., M.B.A., DBA candidate

Abstract

Artificial intelligence (AI) writing assistants generate text based on input from the human user. Writers in regulated industries, such as healthcare, may not gain as much benefit from AI writers due to the requirements for truthful and complete information. An analysis of the output of seven AI writing assistants demonstrated that the texts generated for a list of side effects of a prescription medication (Lipitor) were generally incomplete and inaccurate. Omissions and inaccuracies are problematic and require revisions by the medical writer. Publishing inaccurate healthcare content on social media is serious as it can affect patient outcomes. More than half (59%) of respondents (n=69) said they would be able to tell whether as a human or an AI app had written health-related content. The researcher then showed human-written and AI-written healthcare texts to healthcare professionals (HCPs) and non-HCPs. The study was single-blinded, so the readers did not know the source of the content. Of the human-written texts that were shown to HCPs ($n=236$) and non-HCPs ($n=418$), 55.9% and 54.1% were respectively correctly identified ($p<0.05$). Of the 348 AI-written texts shown to HCPs and 636 to non-HCPs, 59.5% and 50.8% were correctly identified ($p<0.05$).

Keywords: Keywords: *AI Writing Assistant, Artificial Intelligence, GPT-3, Healthcare, Medical writer*

JEL Classification: *M1, M100, M300, M31, M38,*

Introduction

Generative pre-trained transformer 3 (GPT-3) is a language model created by OpenAI capable of generating text in a human-like fashion. It was launched in July 2020 and can generate different types of writing styles. (Kublik and Saboo, 2022) Natural Language Processing (NLP) is the basis for GPT-3, allowing it to understand text and predict the next sequence of words based on its repeated training on a dataset of written content from the internet. (Kublik and Saboo, 2022, Giansiracusa, 2021) The datasets often include "large sets of books, wide internet scrapes, or other easily accessible large text datasets". (Solaiman and Dennison, 2021) The issue with this training is that GPT-3 can also pick up bias (Korngiebel and Mooney, 2021), inaccuracies and conspiracies. (Giansiracusa, 2021) OpenAI, the creators of GPT-3, confirm that bias can be generated when using AI writing assistants using their model: "our API models do exhibit biases that will be reflected in generated text ". (OpenAI, 2020) Since OpenAI launched GPT-3, developers approved by OpenAI have been creating applications to help writers create content based on their output needs. Case studies and discussion threads on social sites such as Reddit highlight how easy it is to create content while using GPT-3 (Giansiracusa, 2021), but very little can be found regarding the use of GPT-3 to generate text in a highly regulated industry, such as healthcare. Medical writers are skilled at communicating up-to-date, scientifically accurate and complete information at the right level based on their readers' experience with the subject. (Sharma, 2010) The use of a GPT-3 model may appeal to busy writers who want to speed up their production. However, risks and benefits must be considered. OpenAI are aware that their product contains risks and admit that these are challenging to identify as the desired behaviour of the tool varies depending on the user's perspective. (Solaiman and Dennison, 2021) Improved patient care is the primary goal for all written healthcare content, and low risk for all stakeholders, including patients and HCPs must be achieved. (Korngiebel and Mooney, 2021) Inaccurate or incomplete healthcare information could be harmful to a patient. It is recognized that language models generate incorrect statements and even fabricate false information. (Zang, D. *et al*., 2022) Due to the growing popularity of AI writing assistants, it is inevitable that with time, a greater number of medical writers will start using them to some capacity. Analyzing case studies where similar texts written by humans and AI machines are compared will help point out the types of errors that can occur and whether readers will be able to determine the source of the text. Better understanding the technology's benefits and challenges will help to identify strategies that will assist medical writers who do use a GPT-3 model to ensure that their final write-up is complete, accurate and transparent for optimal health outcomes. Patient outcome and industry trust is at stake when healthcare information is involved. It's a big responsibility, particularly when published content can be so easily shared to large audiences on social media. As such, the medical writer must carefully weigh whether the use of GPT-3 to product content will help or hinder their overall objective.

Material and Methods

This research included two objectives; i) to quantify the types of errors that can occur when using AI writing assistants for healthcare writing, and ii) to quantify the identification of healthcare text as written by a human or an AI writing assistant by both the general public and HCPs.

1) **Comparing an official list of side effects to AI-generated lists of side effects.**

For the first objective, the list of side effects of Lipitor (atorvastatin) was found in the most recent Lipitor product monograph which had been revised and authorized by Health Canada on November 10, 2021. This served as the control group. Then, the words "List of Lipitor side effects" was input into seven AI writing assistants that offer a paragraph-style output. Sometimes, the words "All medications have side effects, including Lipitor" were included as part of the input if the AI writing assistant requested a longer prompt in order to generate text. The AI writing assistants used were Ryte, WordHero, ContentBot, Texta.ai, Wrytly, Creaitor and Nichesse.. All side effects listed in the output were compared to the list from the product monograph. Consumer-friendly terms that meant the same as the medical term were accepted as an equivalent; "muscle weakness" was accepted as "asthenia", "muscle pain" as "myalgia", "muscle breakdown" as "rhabdomyolysis", "joint pain" as "arthralgia" and "liver damage" or "changes in liver function tests" as "blood creatinine phosphokinase increased". The side effects that were correct, missing or fabricated were counted for the individual AI writing assistants.

2) Quantifying the correct identification of the writing source (human vs. AI writing assistant)

The researcher collected medical texts written by human writers and AI writing assistants.

A. Selecting medical content written by humans:

Medical content written by humans was selected by implementing four Google Chrome searches for the keywords "GERD Overview", "Depression overview", "Obesity overview" and "Flu vaccine safety". The webpages reviewed for selection were based on chronological order as they appeared on the Google Chrome search page. The articles that ranked the highest were reviewed first. If they met the selection criteria, they were chosen. If they did not meet the selection criteria, the next ranked article was reviewed and so on.

The selection criteria for human-written text:

- Must not be an ad nor a promotion of any kind.
- The date of publication or review must be written in the article.
- The date of publication must be prior to June 11, 2020, as this was the initial release date of GPT 3, but not older than 4 years at the time of research.
- Only English sites were reviewed.

Only the introduction of the text was selected for the analysis. The first 90-110 words of the article were chosen in order to avoid cutting off sentences. No editing was performed on spelling, grammatical use, word selection, tone, omissions or additions.

The topics (GERD, depression, obesity and flu vaccine safety) were chosen as information on them was widely published prior to the initial release of GPT-3. Therefore, it is assumed that its content was included as part of the language training dataset.

B. Creating content with AI writing assistants.

The apps Texta.ai, RYTR and WordHero were used to create the AI-written texts. The inputs were "GERD overview", "depression overview", "obesity overview" and "flue vaccine safety". Approximately the first 100 words generated were chosen for the survey.

C. Creating, disseminating, collecting and analyzing survey data

Survey participants could only take the survey once. Participants were identified as belonging to one or more of the following groups: i) medical writer, ii) a healthcare professional (MD, OD, Nurse, Nurse Practitioner, Pharmacist, Dentist), or iii) the general public. Survey participants were presented with four human-written texts and six AI-generated texts. The participants were blinded to the source of the written text.

D. A LinkedIn poll was created to identify readers' perception as to whether medical content is more or less credible when written by human writers vs. artificial intelligence writers.

Results and Discussion

1. Comparing an official list of side effects to AI-generated lists of side effects.

The list of 24 side effects from the Lipitor® product monograph acted as the control group. None of the AI apps captured the entire list of side effects. Between 63% and 100% of the side effects were omitted from the list generated by the AI writing assistants. Between 0 and 12 additional side effects were fabricated by each of the AI apps.

This research affirms that AI writing assistants cannot be relied on to produce factually accurate content. This was expected as OpenAI themselves have published that their GPT-3 model has known risks of bias and fabrication. (OpenAI, 2022)

Table 1: Accuracy and completeness of side effects generated by AI writing assistants compared to those from the product's authorized product monograph

	Ryte	WordHero	ContentBot	Texta.ai	Wrytly	Creaitor	Nichesse
Number of correct side effects (n=24)	4 (17%)	9 (38%)	6 (25%)	2 (8%)	3 (13%)	7 (29%)	0 (0%)
Number of omitted side effects	20 (83%)	15 (63%)	18 (75%)	22 (92%)	21 88%)	17 (71%)	24 (100%)
Number of fabricate	4	4	0	12	4	1	5

d side effects							

2. Quantifying the correct identification of the writing source (human vs. AI writing assistant)

A LinkedIn poll was designed to determine if the readers knew the source of the written content, would it impact their trust it. The responses suggest that readers have greater trust in content written by a human compared to an AI app. When surveyed, 77% (53 out of 69) responded that they would expect the level of credibility of human-written healthcare content as being highly credible (levels 8 to 10) whereas 27% (20 out of 74) responded the same regarding healthcare content written by an AI writing assistant.

A separate LinkedIn poll aimed to find out if people thought they would be able to tell if healthcare copy was written by a human or by an AI writing assistant. The results showed that 59% of people were confident they would be able to tell the difference, whereas 29% did not believe they could and 12% were uncertain.

Respondents (n=164) were asked to read medical texts and identify whether they thought it was written by a human or an artificial intelligence assistant writer. More than half of human-written text shown to HCPs (55.9%) and non-HCPs (54.1%) were correctly identified. There was no significant difference between both groups (Chi-square, $p<0.05$). Similar results were found for healthcare texts written by AI writing assistants; HCPs (59.5%) and non-HCPs (50.8%). There was no significant difference (Chi-square, $p<0.05$) in this scenario either. This study suggests that the ability of HCPs and non-HCPS to make this distinction of the source text was the same. Both groups are able to correctly identify the source approximately half the time. This suggests that healthcare content published on social media would only be correctly recognized about half the time as having been written by either a human or an AI app.

Conclusion

Readers have reason to put more faith in the credibility of healthcare content that is written by humans vs. an AI writing assistant. An analysis of seven AI writing assistants' output of a list of side effects of a well-published prescription product demonstrates that generated output is generally incorrect and incomplete. Some credible information may be produced; however, it may not be the most crucial information. More than half of the actual information is omitted, and falsehoods are created. Although the source of slightly more than half of the human-written and AI-written texts were correctly identified, there was no statistical difference between the correct responses by the HCPs and non-HCPs ($p<0.05$). This demonstrates how easy it could be for AI-written healthcare text to be perceived and trusted as credible information written by a human. In the age of social media where misinformation can be easily shared to a large audience, there should be guidelines to help medical writers to properly use GPT-3 apps. They can be useful tools in terms of speeding up the writing process, but they have been shown to lack the ability to produce accurate and complete data in healthcare. Based on the known risks of GPT-3 and the sensitivity required in medical content, it seems that the use of an AI writing assistant in the medical writing field may be fraught unless the human writer is willing to take considerable time to review and update the generated text for complete truthfulness. Overall, the medical writer must carefully weigh the pros and cons of using a GPT-3 model and understand its limitations in order to produce content that will benefit patient outcomes and push towards creating trust. Despite the growing popularity of AI writing assistants, they are not yet in a position to replace human writers with scientific knowledge, attention to detail and delivery expertise.

This research is a single analysis based on a minuscule fraction of the GPT-3 model. More research is required in order to provide medical writers with adequate strategies to allow them to benefit from the use of an AI writing assistant without risking the quality of the final written product. GPT-4, the successor of GPT-3, was rumoured to launch by the end of Summer 2022 but it still has not at the time that this paper was written. (Romero, 2022) Studies will be required on the updated GPT-4 model.

Acknowledgements

The research for this paper was created within the scope of the LIGS University Doctorate of Business Administration program.

References

Giansiracuso, N. (2021). How Algorithms Create and Prevent Fake News. Exploring the Impacts of Social Media, Deepfakes, GPT-3 and More. (1st ed.). Apress. https://doi.org/10.1007/978-1-4842-7155-1

Korngiebel, D.M., Mooney, S.D. (2021). Considering the possibilities and pitfalls of Generative Pre-trained Transformer 3 (GPT-3) in healthcare delivery. *npj Digital Medicine*, 4(93), https://doi.org/10.1038/s41746-021-00464-x.

Kublik, S., Saboo, S. (2022). Building Innovative NLP Products Using Large Language Models. O'Reilly Media, Inc.

OpenAI. (2020, June 11). *OpenAI API*. https://openai.com/blog/openai-api/

OpenAI. (2020). *Training language models to follow instructions with human feedback.* https://cdn.openai.com/papers/Training_language_models_to_follow_instructions_with_human_feedback.pdf

Sharma, S. (2010). How to Become a Competent Medical Writer? *PICR*, 1(1),

Solaiman, I., Dennison, C. (2021, December 6-14). Process for Adapting Language Models to Society (PALMS) with Values-Targeted Datasets. 35th Conference on Neural Information Processing Systems. [Conference presentation]. NeurIPS 2021, Sydney, Australia.

Romero, A. (2022, April 17). *GPT-4 Is Coming Soon. Here's What We Know About It*. https://towardsdatascience.com/gpt-4-is-coming-soon-heres-what-we-know-about-it-64db058cfd45

Upjohn Canada ULC, Pfizer Ireland Pharmaceuticals. (2021, Nov. 10). *Product Monograph. PrLipitor®*. https://www.pfizer.ca/sites/default/files/202112/LIPITOR_PM_EN_253694_2021.11.10.pdf

Zhang, D. *et al*. (2022, March). *The AI Index 2022 Annual Report. Stanford University. Human-Centered Artificial Intelligence.* https://hai.stanford.edu/research/ai-index-2022

Contact information

Name of the author: Natalie Bourré

Affiliation (University): LIGS University

Email: Marketing4health@yahoo.ca

Fake News and New Social Media and the Impact on Women Entrepreneurship

Carolina M. Billings

Abstract

This paper aims to identify the impact of fake news on a women-businesses operating on social media platforms. The findings show that men's and women's perception of difficulty in identifying fake news is similar. In contrast, women are more concerned than men about the harmful effects of misinformation on society. This article's main objective is to investigate users' perception of fake news, as well as identify the criteria on which their recognition strategies are based and the effect on their choice of the social media platform for their business strategy as well as the correlation between fake news content and the changing demographic of platforms such as the boomerizing of Facebook, and aging of Instagram and TikTok and the migration to new platforms. The results are based on the analysis of interviews where participants were asked about their competence in determining the veracity of the information, misinformation vs disinformation and their ability to identify false content. Their consideration of changing their existing social media platform for emerging new social media as a result. Benefits are related to a better understanding of the effect of algorithms on business marketing as a result of mitigating fake news.

Keywords: *Algorithms and Marketing, Fake News, Gender and Management, New social media, Women Entrepreneurship*

JEL Classification: *M1, M3, 035*

Introduction

What is Fake News, and who decides what and when is fake? According to the Center for Information Technology & Society (University of California Santa Barbara, 2022) *The term fake news means "news articles that are intentionally and verifiably false" [1] designed to manipulate people's perceptions of real facts, events, and statements. It's about information presented as news that is known by its promoter to be false based on facts that are demonstrably incorrect or statements or events that verifiably did not happen. Fake news "is fabricated information that mimics news media content in form but...lack(s) the news media's editorial norms and processes for ensuring the accuracy and credibility of information" [2]. It overlaps with misinformation (false or misleading information) and disinformation (false information purposely spread to mislead people)*. (University of California Santa Barbara, 2022) the challenge of this definition is the concept of *"news articles that are intentionally and verifiably false."*

Calling out *Fake News* as we understand it today became popular in politics during the 2016 US presidential elections (Gentzkow, 2017)where anything that did not appear to serve or show the candidate in a bad light immediately got labelled fake news to *discredit and move on*. However, perhaps the articles in question were intentionally bias and lacking of journalistic due process but, at the time of the labelling and not been verified as false. Therefore, calling out fake news without verification could equate to falsehood as the articles or information in question. The research question for this paper is: How do social media platform efforts to mitigate *Fake News* affect social media-based entrepreneurs?

The evolution of the News

Who is the media now?

Social Media platforms have become a haven for the dissemination of misinformation; however there are things to consider. 1. *Traditional or main street media* relies strongly on social media platforms for engagement and distribution (Gaskins, 2012) and 2) Traditional/Main Stream media also relies heavily on *citizen journalism, blogs and video footage.* (Bruns, 2009). And if we include the concept of disinformation under the fake news spectrum, one cannot avoid *compromised* or bias news from mainstream media as a result of either their clear political alignments, i.e., *CNN vs Fox News* in the United Estates but also one must consider the news outlets sponsors, stakeholders i.e., big pharma, big tech. "Without *citizen journalism* to hold accountability to power, there would have been No George Floyd" (Sloan, 2022), a powerful example of the good side of social media and how it has opened the doors for the *democratization* of information. For every unverified *citizen report,* there is now a spotlight on the truth for the unrepresented. (Sloan, 2022).

Pivotal points of the evolution of sources of dissemination of information.

In 1967's in his article "*The medium is the message,*" McLuhan concluded that *"the personal and social consequences of any medium – that is, of any extension of ourselves – result from the new scale that is introduced into our affairs by each extension of ourselves or by any new technology"* (McLuhan, 1967). Today's reality as stated by CNN's Brian Stelter's during his exit broadcast after the cancellation of the show *Reliable Sources*, a show *about the media within a media outlet* purportedly holding *itself* accountable. Brian Stelter states, *"media is evolving at a dizzying speed, the biggest change is people carrying super computers in their pockets ready to capture events as they unfold...the media is not the enemy of the people, the media is the people."* (CNN, 2022). Are *We* the people now the medium?

Demographics and the choice of social media

Not all fake news affects social platforms equally. During research interviews, interviewees were asked: *Users' perception of fake news, as well as identify the criteria on which their recognition strategies are based as well as their competence in determining the veracity of the information, misinformation vs disinformation and their ability to identify false content.*

All respondents shared similar demographics within their level of education: *all respondents have a post-graduate college degree and operate a service-based enterprise using social media as part of their business strategy. On a scale of 1 to 10, all respondents felt competent, rating themselves at an 8+ of their ability to spot questionable content* (Hall, 2022) (Herschorn, 2022) (Magill, 2022) (Skalli, 2022) (Wagner, 2022). *All respondents cited a) using multiple sources, including mainstream media, for*

their source of news and b) Following the story back to its source and considering source biases and influencing stakeholders especially regarding medical news. All respondents cited LinkedIn as their primary social media/network platform choice. All respondents rated the quality of information and participants as trustworthy within the LinkedIn network.
(Hall, 2022) (Herschorn, 2022) (Magill, 2022) (Skalli,2022) (Wagner, 2022)
There were, however two answers that highlighted the question: What is the influence of demographics and culture on the acceptance and interpretation of fake news through social media.

Fake News: Misinformation vs Disinformation & Citizen Journalism

Because social media is a public platform, anyone—including news outlets—can post anything without being accountable for fact-checking. It's left to users to distinguish misinformation vs. disinformation in their feeds. (Intuit Mail Chimp, 2022)

Two respondents provided a unique perspective regarding perceived misinformation vs disinformation and the role of citizen journalism as news content within social media channels. To properly represent the significance of their answers, we must explore two concepts: *Misinformation vs disinformation and Citizen Journalism*. What differentiates misinformation from disinformation is the *intent of the person or outlet sharing it* (Filippo Menczer, 2016). In the previously cited study from Indiana University, misinformation is classified as *"false or misleading content including hoaxes, conspiracy theories, fabricated reports, click-bait headlines, and even satire."* Misinformation is not deliberately intended to deceive. Instead, it aims to shape or change public opinion on a topic. Disinformation can be spread using many of the same tactics as misinformation—hoaxes, click-bait, and frabricated reports. Disinformation is created to deceive. (Intuit MailChimp, 2022). Lastly citizen journalism: *Citizen journalism is a media concept that refers to ordinary people's journalistic activities. It means citizens themselves report the issues confronting them. Citizen journalism has enabled people to raise their voice on what they feel need attention. These people are, thus, termed citizen journalists. Citizen journalists or amateur reporters are none but the general audience, that is, viewers, readers and listeners of mainstream media*. (Noor, 2020) As observed by Alex Bruns "*New competitors with the products of the journalism industry frequently take professional journalists themselves to task where their standards have appeared to have slipped, and are beginning to match the news industry's incumbents in terms of insight and informational value: recent studies have shown, for example, that avid Daily Show viewers are as if not better informed about the U.S. political process as those who continue to follow mainstream print or television news"* (Bruns, 2009)

Fake News as a Spectrum

During my research interviews, two perspectives highlighted a deeper reflection regarding not only *who* is reporting it but *what* is being reported by citizens and its impact on Main Stream Media. Simone Sloan Rph, MBA, mentioned the *consequences and responsibility* of citizen journalism. *"Although without citizen journalism movements such as Black Lives Matter would not have been able to provide the evidence of the real-life events faced by underrepresented communities, those too must be viewed with an eye of skepticism and conduct due diligence. I can look at two news reporting of the same incident using the same footage and have it be manipulated to mean different things, however, many times it is only being reported as a result of the live footage, which has been made public uncensored. Without citizen journalism, there would have been no George Floyd"* (Sloan, 2022)

Another perspective of citizen journalism impacting Fake News is the dissemination of information through social media uncensored by government regulations. Y. Skalli highlighted the perspective of East versus West sensitivities regarding freedom of the press in highly active geo-political regions outside of North America (Skalli, 2022) *"In places where official sources are not trusted, social media is relied on and perhaps given an element of credibility as it gets distributed through trusted sources from people to people. The misinformation comes about perhaps not intentionally but as a result of the interpretation given as it spreads through social media communities. Commentary taking a more critical role than the source or validity. A personal strategy, then is more about critical thinking and a personal mindset as to how vulnerable you are at believing what is being reported by people through social media. The most important way for me to try to determine whether content seems fake is for me to evaluate my own cultural biases related to the topic.* In her New York Times Article titled *Revolution-Facebook Style* A. Shapiro reported: *"As the street protests went on, young Egyptians also were mobilizing and venting their anger over Gaza on what would, until recently, have seemed an unlikely venue: Facebook, the social-networking site. In most countries in the Arab world, Facebook is now one of the 10 most-visited Web sites, and in Egypt, it ranks third, after Google and Yahoo.* (Shapero, 2009)

Intersectionality of Business and Personal use of Social Media

The Great Resignation (Serenko, 2022) has accelerated the rate at which women have chosen to start their service-based businesses. More than 40% of all employees were thinking about leaving their jobs at the beginning of 2021, and as the year went on, workers quit in unprecedented numbers. (Microsoft, 2021) This movement and opt-in of social media platforms has the ability to alter the demographics and the very nature of a platform. For example, the aging of Facebook by the percentage of *Boomer* users. *Aging* is also currently being experienced by Instagram and TikTok. *TikTok has previously been seen as a network for primarily Gen Z, but now just 47% of TikTok users are between ages 10-29, compared to 62% last year. The platform's user base is aging up with 42% of users now aged 30-49. If this trend continues, we could see something like the Boomer takeover of Facebook.* (Intuit Mail Chimp, 2022) Without a marketing strategy, understanding of emerging/changing platforms and a robust following, entrepreneurs can easily burn through resources leading to failure to launch. Our research shows that by *leveraging the aggregate*, women entrepreneurs can accelerate their presence, understand emerging platforms, increase engagement and monetization of their services to result in their ability to become financially independent, establish their brand presence and refresh their social marketing strategy for growth. As an example of the use of aggregate during our research, the six interviews conducted represent business-to-business consultants each representing an average of 50 clients. Therefore, observation data for this paper is based on approximately 300 women entrepreneurs.

Social Media is not just Social.

For women entrepreneurs there is an ongoing intersectionality between business and personal use *"my personal social media is my business social media. My brand is about a lifestyle I live authentically using social media as social proof"* (Magill, 2022). Most women-owned service-based businesses rely on social media platforms to market their business. The ease of entry, familiarity of a particular social platform and perceived quick monetization can become a source of frustration when taken from the personal to business. In her book *(Not) Getting Paid for What you Love*, B. E. Duffy identifies the lure of ease calling women by the millions to social media entrepreneurship only to find dissolution. *"These content creators, I came to realize, were motivated by the wider culture's siren to call to get paid to do what you love. But what they experienced often fell short of the promise...the rest are un(der)-paid, remunerated with the deferred promise of "exposure" or "visibility." "A grueling balancing act is required, On that I explore thought the lest of "aspirational labor". (Duffy, 2017)*

The low barrier to entry often results in bypassing fundamental business foundations such as proof of concept, unique value proposition, business plans, marketing strategies, and market analysis to name a few. All these are under their control. What most self-professed women digital entrepreneurs often underestimate are the challenges out of their control within social media platforms.

Changing Logarithms & Handling of Fake News by Platform's Leadership

On a recent interview of Facebook Founder Mark Zuckerberg on the Joe Rogan podcast (Zuckerberg, 2020), dated two days from the date of this citation had received 2.4M views on YouTube, *"When we take down something that we were not supposed to, it is like the worst." How do you discern asked Rogan: How do you know when someone is real or not? This is the big argument between Elon Musk and Tweeter. He was asked what is the percentage of bots and fake accounts he was told 5% to which Elon responded it has to be much, much higher than that." "When we look at a page, there are a whole bunch of signals we do not rely just on AI...it is all a trade-off. We could be totally more aggressive catch 100% of the bad guys but in the process take down the good guys or we could be more lenient and say the cost of taking down any number of good guys is too high so we opt to let in some bad guys in". "For big accounts we make sure we know who the administrator is" "when an account is put on hold because it has breached policy it gets sent to a review board".* When pressed how Facebook handles controversial stories that end up being true, Zuckerberg admitted *"the process isn't perfect" "it sucks probably in the same way of going through a criminal trial but in the end proving that you are innocent...in the end you are free."* (Zuckerberg, 2020)

How is currently being solved

LinkedIn although not considered a social media platform is the digital media networking of choice for business-to-business consultants 86.6% of our interviewees identified LinkedIn as their networking, marketing and prospecting platform of choice. 13% of respondents identified Facebook as their primary Social Media platform of choice for business and personal. 100% of the respondents identified changes in *Logarithms* as the number one reason for business interruption. *"For some marketers, they're like little data puzzles just waiting to be solved. But if you're like most businesses trying to tackle social media, they're a sort of boogeyman. The great "unknown" that's holding your content down. Algorithms might seem helpful and mostly harmless to the average social customer, helping sift through content and deliver only "relevant" content rather than random posts. However, marketers that don't fully understand what algorithms are or how they work will find themselves facing a constant struggle."* (Barnhart, 2021) Overall, the experts interviewed rated their client's technical abilities a 5.5 out of 10 relying almost exclusively on consultants such as themselves or hiring social media experts to guide them through.

Research Data and Methodology

The research presented on this paper has been conducted by The Hive Consulting Group Inc. (THGC) a Toronto based Boutique Management Consulting firm located in Ontario, Canada with an international clientele.

Its niche market is incubating, growing and accelerating women's professional success as a closed consortium of women professional corporations, service-based enterprises and brands for 10 years. Methods of data collection for qualitative research, include observations, co-creation of initiatives, textual and visual analysis, book publishing, video production and individual and group interviews. The community withing THCG operating as *Powerful Women Today* consists of 50 women entrepreneurs operating as a consortium of business-to-business consultants operating as Ph.D.'s, Master level clinicians, licensed professionals, self-made millionaires and subject matter experts collectively servicing thousands of regular clients within the consolidated portfolios in modalities such as finance, law, relationships, coaching, vocational, wellness, business consulting and lifestyle. The consortium members perform the role leadership as *Mentor Experts working as an aggregate* to the open opt-in Powerful Women Today community of approximately 500,000 globally. Interviews were conducted in a Semi-structured video format consisting of several key questions that helped to define the areas to be explored, but also allowed the interviewee to diverge in order to pursue an idea or response in more detail. *The flexibility of this approach, particularly compared to structured interviews, also allows for the discovery or elaboration of information that is important to participants but may not have previously been thought of as pertinent by the research team.* (Gill, 2008)

Results and Discussion

- Users' perception of fake news, as well as identify the criteria on which their recognition strategies are based:
  - 100% of respondents rated themselves 8/10 at being able to identify fake content on news.
  - 100% of respondents rated themselves 8+/10 at having a strategy for recognition. Raging from *sources* (Sloan, 2022) *research* (Herschorn, 2022) to *correlating multiple sources* (Magill, 2022) (Wagner, 2022).
- Competence in determining the veracity of the information, *misinformation vs disinformation* and their ability to identify false content: *"News have evolved there are so many so-called experts specially regarding pharmaceutical, so many channels it fully understanding sources, biases, who is sponsoring it, the motivations behind it and expert's credentials."* (Sloan, 2022) *"Fake news is nothing new. It is as much about omission as it is about bias."* (Hall, 2022)

- 100% of respondents rated themselves 8+/10 in their competence of being able to discern misinformation from disinformation.

- Understanding Logarithms and business disruption as a result of platforms mitigating fake content: *"There is no communication when changes are made to a platform. It seems Facebook is both the platform most affected and the one that keeps changing the most. Accounts were being penalized for large number of contacts that do not engage. Visibility went down, they are now wanting to make sure you engage first, share second. Creators with fan/business pages who had amassed large number of followers experience their visibility on their business page disappeared overnight unless ads are being purchased. It is the lack of communication that is the most disruptive not so much the change in policy or practice."* (Hall, 2022) during the Joe Rogan Experience's podcast Mark Zuckerberg stated that one strategy to mitigate fake content is to have *"paid advertising by business accounts whose administrator is known"* (Zuckerberg, 2022) for most small businesses that relied on organic visibility of their contents, paid advertising needs to be significant in order to make a consistent difference in their business. This is most of the time not affordable. *"Lately the biggest algorithm threat is accounts being put on "Facebook Jail" that are not creating bad content, a recent example is a business owner's account being put on hold over "nudity". It was a business account with no images nor copy that is remotely near it. So, you have to wonder, what is getting caught on these nets? What are they really looking for?"* (Hall, 2022)

- Changing demographic of platforms such as the *boomerizing of Facebook*, and aging of Instagram and TikTok and the migration to new platforms. Changes in functionality of existing platforms. Shifting of demographics was rated 7/10 by S. Wagner during our interview. *"It is not about where you want to be but where your clients are moving to"* (Wagner, 2022) *"Platforms seems to be expanding their functionality to compete with each other. YouTube now has TikTok like short clips, Instagram now wants more Video like YouTube, LinkedIn offers audio now like Clubhouse. Even Facebook and LinkedIn's dashboards look alike now. It takes a lot for someone to switch to a new social media platform."* (Herschorn, 2022)

Conclusion

The demographic we serve are highly educated, remember *professional journalism* and are not technology savvy. Based on the Diffusion of Innovation modelling (Rogers, 2003) six interviewees representing 500+ entrepreneurs using social media as the key channel for their brand's message distribution are classified as a *late majority* (Hall, 2022) (Magill, 2022) (Herschorn, 2022) (Wagner, 2022) in their likelihood to embrace New Social Media Channels. A greater understanding of the role social media plays in the marketing and sales funnel as well as the understanding that their *following* is not a *client list.* Social media is a *meeting/prospecting place* and a good place for *social proof* for business and personal brands not a place to *stay and run* a service-based business. *"Social influence rises with the number of influence sources, but the proposed relationship varies across theories, situations, and research paradigms."* (MacCoun, 2012) Relying on Social Media platforms as your entire marketing, branding and engagement strategy is too volatile and vulnerable for businesses. The changes in algorithms seem to be the primary source of *business interruption* and *concern* more so than fake news or content. Overall, the second biggest point of vulnerability for women business owners is remaining 100% on social media once they have converted their clients, relying on it as their *technology strategy* for community, business development and engagement. Followers or contacts are not *owned* by the business owners. Overnight and without reason social media platforms such as Facebook, Instagram, TikTok and Tweeter to name the most popular and free to users, can be shut down overnight or close user accounts at will. LinkedIn as a paid platform focusing on professionals and business owners seems to be the least affected by Fake News, bots, and fake profiles. LinkedIn has encouraged users to bring more social and casual networking engagement, however, the membership itself self-audits and censors non-LinkedIn-like behaviour seen on other platforms. Changes in logarithms should not shut down a business that has a clear *value ladder or sales funnel* leading them *away* from reliance on social media for their communication and engagement with their clients/list. This really ought to be done via CRM's, email campaigns, newsletters and regularly scheduled events that bring the community together and provide *live* brand experience and engagement.

References

Barnhart, B. (2021, March 26). *Everything you need to know about social media algorithms*. Retrieved from Sprout Social: https://sproutsocial.com/insights/social-media-algorithms/

Bruns, A. (2009). *QUT*. Retrieved from News blogs and citizen journalism: New directions for e-Journalism: https://eprints.qut.edu.au/32539/

CNN. (2022, 08). *CNN Business Reliable Sources Broadcast*. Retrieved from CNN.com: https://www.cnn.com/videos/media/2022/08/21/brian-stelter-goodbye-final-reliable-sources-episode-rs-vpx.cnn/video/playlists/business-media/

Duffy, B. E. (2017). *(Not) Getting Paid for What You Love. Gender, Social Media and Aspirational Work.* New Haven: Yale Publishing.

Filippo Menczer, I. U. (2016, April). The Spread of Misinformation in Social Media. *WWW '16 Companion: Proceedings of the 25th International Conference Companion on World Wide Web*, Pages 717 https://doi.org/10.1145/2872518.2890092. Retrieved from UCLA: https://www.ipam.ucla.edu/abstract/?tid=13275&pcode=CAWS3

Gaskins, B. (2012). Internet News: Is It a Replacement for Traditional Media Outlets? *The International Journal of Press/Politics*, 2012;17(2):190-213.

Gentzkow, H. A. (2017). Social Media and Fake News in the 2016 Election. *Journal of Economic Perspectives*, Volume 31, Number 2—Spring 2017—Pages 211–236.

Gill, P. S. (2008). Methods of data collection in qualitative research: interviews and focus groups. *Br Dent J 204, 291–295 (2008)*, https://doi.org/10.1038/bdj.2008.192.

Hall, S. (2022, 08 24). Social Media Expert. (C. M. Billings, Interviewer)

Herschorn, M. (2022, 08 23). Journalist & Media Expert. (C. M. Billings, Interviewer)

Intuit Mail Chimp. (2022, 08). *Intuit Mail Chimp*. Retrieved from Marketing Library: https://mailchimp.com/en-ca/resources/fake-news-on-social-media/

Intuit MailChimp. (2022, 08). *Marketing Library*. Retrieved from IntuitMailChimp.com: https://mailchimp.com/en-ca/resources/fake-news-on-social-media/

MacCoun, R. J. (2012). The burden of social proof: Shared thresholds and social influence. *Pshychological Reivew*, Vol 119(2), Apr 2012, 345-372.

Magill, D. E. (2022, 08 25). PhD. (C. M. Billings, Interviewer)

McLuhan, M. &. (1967). *The Medium Is The Messsage* . New York: New York, 123(1), 126-12.

Microsoft. (2021, March). *The Next Great Disruption Is Hybrid Work – Are We Ready?* Retrieved from www.microsoft.com.: https://www.microsoft.com/en-us/worklab/work-trend-index/hybrid-work

Rabia Noor (Islamic University of Science and Technology, I. (2020). *Citizen Journalism: New-Age Newsgathering.* Retrieved from IGI Global: https://www.igi-global.com/chapter/citizen-journalism/246688

Rogers, E. (2003). *Diffusion of Innovations.* New York: Free Press.

Serenko, A. (2022). The Great Resignation: the great knowledge exodus or the onset of the Great Knowledge Revolution? *Journal of Knowledge Management*, Ahead of Print.

Shapero, S. (2009, January). *Revolution, Facebook-Style*. Retrieved from NYTimes.com:

https://www.nytimes.com/2009/01/25/magazine/25bloggers-t.html

Skalli, Y. (2022, 08 26). Fake News and New Social Media Research interview. (C. M. Billings, Interviewer)

Sloan, S. (2022, 08 18). RpH, MBA . (C. M. Billings, Interviewer)

University of California Santa Barbara. (2022, 08 25). *Center for Information Technology & Society*. Retrieved from Fake News Menu: https://www.cits.ucsb.edu/fake-news/what-is-fake-news

University of California Santa Barbara. (2022, 08). *CITS*. Retrieved from University of California Santa Barbara: https://www.cits.ucsb.edu

Zuckerberg, M. (2020, 08). The Joe Rogan Experience Podcast. (J. Rogan, Interviewer)

Contact information

Name of the author: Carolina M. Billings
Affiliation (University): LIGS University
Email: Carolina.billings@gmail.com

Exploring weaknesses in Facebook's algorithm and Cambridge Analytica

Jiri Medlen, Patrick Medlen, Lenka Sulova

Abstract

The study aimed to explore weaknesses in Facebook's algorithm. Today, politicians are screaming that Social Media is responsible for the polarization of the U.S. population. Is this an accurate statement? What exactly is responsible for the polarization? In an attempt to gain some answers, we concentrated on Facebook, where we looked at the technology used and examined the revenue model. This study has two parts. One of the most important parts was an experiment with the Facebook News section to illustrate the problem we face using Social Media. This issue is not only limited to particular news channels, as the ability for anyone to reach millions of users regardless of the quality of the news they produce and the blatant abuse of the first amendment also poses significant problems. The second part is regarding the involvement of Cambridge Analytica in referendum manipulation related to the UK leaving the European Union. Finally, we came up with some recommendations to implement in this scenario.

Keywords: *Facebook, Meta, social media*

JEL Classification: *C10, C12, C90, D12*

Introduction

The Internet is one of the most significant inventions of this century. The Internet has wholly democratized knowledge, the power to sell and publish. The selling and publishing privileges were shifted from a few privileged to everybody.

How did it all start? It started with ARPANET (The U.S. Advanced Research Projects Agency Network) in 1968 (Wright, 2021). ARPANET was heavily used for research by universities and was the Internet's predecessor. At that time, the communication protocols were weak and not standardized. The breakthrough came with the invention of TCP/IP (Transfer Control Protocol/Internetwork Protocol), and on January 1st, 1983, we could consider the Internet's birthday (ARPANET switched to TCP/IP) (Usg, n.d.).

The beginning was hard. We could handle mostly text with Gopher and file transfer with FTP (File Transfer Protocol). To connect to the server, Telnet was and still is a must. The email significantly improved, and we could use Usenet newsgroups (moderated). IRC (Internet Relay Chat) was another outstanding achievement. The real change came with Hypertext transfer protocol — a.k.a. "The Web" and Netscape's browser, which could handle images. The additional improvement came from a Uniform Resource Locator (URL) for the servers. However, it is hard for humans to remember numbers like http://198.15.93.98 better would be a text, and another invention solved that. The Domain Name System (DNS) turns domain names into IP addresses.

How do you find the servers? The following invention came quickly, and the answer was directory Yahoo. It was better but not great. Search engines (Infoseek, Alta Vista, and later Google (Wikipedia, 2022d)) started to pop up. The next significant milestone was online shopping, and eBay and later Amazon was born.

Innovation riched Social Media space, and Myspace started in 2003, and Friendster started in 2002 (Wikipedia, 2022a) were created (Viktor, 2022). This started the Social Media (SM) revolution. The biggest name in the SM space today is Facebook (FB) (today Meta), and FB started in 2004 (Wikipedia, 2022c). Let us look at the most prominent names, Google, Twitter, and Facebook.

How is Google making money? Google revolutionized the advertisement space (Leonard, 2022), and most of the revenue is from Google Ads. Google is a search engine so that users will perform a search, review results quickly, and move on with the task. Google does not own the content. It will index whatever web server has. Good or bad, true or false, is entirely irrelevant for Google.

How is Twitter making money? Twitter makes money from advertisements and data selling (Investopedia, 2022).

How is Facebook making money? Most of the revenue is from Facebook and Instagram apps (Franek, 2021). Unlike with Google, users publish on Facebook's platform; in some sense, Facebook can monitor the content if required. At this point, Facebook is operating under the belief that people are good and they would self-monitor themselves and publish only quality documents. So it is the end user's responsibility. This is an absolutely naive premise. Today platforms like Facebook and Twitter gave ordinary people the power, the ability, and the freedom to publish. With freedom comes big responsibility. People should publish only true and quality posts. Only experts should give, e.g., medical advice. Today it is not the truth, and everybody can talk about whatever. Social media is a significant junkyard.

Can Facebook or Twitter remove any posts, and by doing it, is Facebook or Twitter violating the First Amendment? The First Amendment protects free speech in public property or forums that the public or government owes. Facebook is a private company that can remove posts that are not written according to its published guidelines (Grimaldi, 2022).

Does the First Amendment protect false statements? The First Amendment's purpose is to further the pursuit of truth; therefore, untruth is not protected (Vile, 2009). However, sometimes it might be impossible to distinguish truth from untruths, so untruths may sometimes be unpunished. Why is it so hard to find the truth? Let us look at the absolute truth. Does it exist? One example of absolute truth is "no round squares" (Wikipedia, 2021a).

Let us try other examples. Who is right?

(1a) A religious person would claim that God exists. (1b) The atheist would claim that God does not exist. (2a) Wine is good for you. (2b) Wine is bad for you. (3a) Vaccination is good for you. (3b) Vaccination is bad for you.

Why is it so hard to monitor the quality of the posts (OECD, 2022), and why Twitter and Facebook cannot remove them so easily? How can we detect fake news using machine learning (ML)? ML could help. However, it requires supervised learning and, therefore, manual labeling. The main issue is that the labeling team might sometimes have difficulty distinguishing between fake news and what is not. After we have enough examples, we could use, e.g., Naïve Bayes or SVM for the modeling (training and testing with a typical split of 70/30 or 80/20). We used Python and Anaconda distribution 3.7. Another great possibility is to use R (RPubs - Text Analysis using SVM, 2019) or RapidMiner (great for non-programmers with drag&drop functionality). We used classification, and it is 2 class problem (Fake post-YES/NO). The basic idea is straightforward. Some words will be more prominent for each class. Well. How about other examples (Table 1)?

Post	Fake post Y/N	Notes
I saw Jesus walking on the Golden gate bridge.	YES	The probability of this event is very low => most likely fake news
The mortality rate of COVID-19 Omicron variant BA.5 is increasing.	?	This is hard to tell – only the author can tell for sure.
Pelosi's Plane Lands in Taiwan Despite China Warning.	NO	

Table 1. Provides examples of some hypothetical posts: source, the author.

Why are people writing fake news? What is their motivation (British Council, n.d.).)?

1. Feed the ego. The author thinks he/she is brighter than the rest of us.
2. Politically motivated. He/she is trying to incriminate opponents. Alternatively, simply divide and conquer the society. Russia and China are manipulating elections in the US.
3. Simply for a profit.

What is selling more fear versus non-fear news?
Unfortunately, the latest research confirms that fear is the best-selling brand today. It is probably still because of our survival instinct (UN, 2019).

Facebook and Twitter are making money from advertisements, and their main objective is to try to please the users and tell them what they want to hear so they stay on the platform as long as possible so FB and Twitter can to serve them more and more adds. The basic technology they are using is the Recommendation engines.

The study's objective is to investigate the explore weaknesses in Facebook's algorithm. The author uses multiple techniques to answer some of the complex questions. It is a mix of reviewing Internet articles and running a simple Experiment.

The Review of the Internet articles

Recommendation engines:

The purpose is to understand better recommendation engines and weaknesses.

Run one Experiment

The purpose of the experiments is to see the performance of Facebook recommendation engines' algorithm.

Cambridge Analytica:

The purpose is to understand the involvement of Cambridge Analytica in referendum manipulation related to the UK leaving the European Union.

Material and Methods

This section covers the used methods and methodology.

Material:

NA

Methods:

Experiment: The experiment aims to understand Facebook's recommendation news engine.

Model and Data

This section covers used models and collected data.

Literature review - Recommendation engines:

The purpose is to understand better recommendation engines their strengths and weaknesses.

The recommendation engines will recommend the users similar content based on the past and the click history. Recommendation engines have several issues.

The first one is a Cold start. When the user is new, the Recommendation engines have no idea what content to offer. The solution can be as simple as random articles or the most popular articles. If I have access to gender and age, I can offer the most popular articles per gender and age group.

The second issue is that Recommendation engines will put the user in the box, which is tough to get out of. In the old days, newspapers often had several antagonistic opinions so that the user would get a better picture. Recommendation engines will not do that; they start feeding the user only articles with one opinion. Moreover, the recommendation engine is responsible for society's polarization. The best way is to illustrate it on a real example and run a simple experiment using Facebook news.

Literature review - Cambridge Analytica:

The Brexit referendum was on 23 June 2016 (Duffield, 2021), and the Leave EU Vote share was 51.9% votes (17,410,742) (BBC, 2016) vs. Remain in EU Vote share was 48.1% votes (16,141,241). The difference is 1,269,501. Electorate was 46,501,241 = 72.2%. Before we look at Cambridge Analytica and its involvement in Brexit, we had to get a feel for Brexit in general (Table 2).

Source	Google Query	Result
Google	"remain in EU"	630,000
Google	"leave EU"	330,000
Facebook	"remain in EU" site:facebook.com	5,400
Facebook	"leave EU" site:facebook.com	91,000
Twitter	"remain in EU" site:twitter.com	11,000
Twitter	"leave EU" site:twitter.com	107,000

Table 2. Brexit queries executed 8/11/2022: source, the author.

From the results, we saw that Twitter and Facebook are for Brexit.

We zoomed in on Facebook (Table 3).

Source	URL	Result
Facebook	https://www.facebook.com/leaveeuofficial/	949,989 likes
Facebook	https://www.facebook.com/remainineu/	2,292 likes

Table 3. Brexit likes extracted 8/11/2022: source, the author.

Facebook users statistics.

Question	Answer
How many users does FB have globally?	As of April 2022, FB has 2.936 billion users (KEMP, 2022). As of 2016, FB has 1.86 billion users (Fiegerman, 2017). As of April 2022, FB has 1.960 billion active users (KEMP, 2022) = 66%.

How many users does FB have in the UK?	As of June 2022, FB has 55.8 million users from the UK (Statista, 2022). As of 2016, FB has 31 million users from the UK (AVOCADO, 2020) = 2%.

Table 4. FB user stats: source, the author.

How is it possible that we saw such disproportion between "Leave EU" and "Remain in EU" likes, and what is the involvement of Cambridge Analytica? Whistleblower Christopher Wylie linked Cambridge Analytica to a pro-Brexit group headed by Boris Johnson, which paid AggregateIQ (AIQ) £625,000 via BeLeave for an online campaign (Martin, 2018a).

Cambridge Analytica harvested FB data from 87 million accounts globally and 70.6 million from the US (Martin, 2018; Wikipedia, 2022e) = 4.6% globally => ~1.74 million UK accounts (assuming random sampling) => Cambridge Analytica harvested ~1.15 million active FB users in the UK in the year 2016. In June 2016, approximately 1/3 of UK voters were undecided (Staiger, 2016). Cambridge Analytica could influence using personal ads 1/3) from 1.15 million active FB users = ~383k users. The open (click) rate is relatively low (conversion rate is even lower), approximately 4% (Mailchimp n.d.), and Cambridge Analytica is adding a

10-20% lift in open rate compared to regular ads (Laterza, 2021). If we calculate a very favorable conversion rate of 25%, we could get 95.75k users. We used PERT = (O + 4M + P)/6=9.3% model (Bell, 2022) where Most Likely=7%, Optimistic=25%, Pessimistic=3%. The number is relatively low to make a difference. Plus, according to Lyle Ungar, a University of Pennsylvania professor, the conversion rate of political ads is very low (Merrill, 2022), so the conversion rate of 25%, is probably super optimistic 9.3% is more likely.

However, it could be a multi-channel effect. It is essential to look at the advertisement financing, where "Leave EU" spent £4.45 million on ads vs. "Remain in EU" spent £1.91 million only (Statista, 2021). The central issue is the fact that "Remain in EU" was able to get only 42% of the funds of "Leave EU".

Experiment - Recommendation engines:

The purpose of the Experiment is to understand Facebook's recommendation news engine. Due to time constrain, we used only one topic to explore Facebook's recommendation news engine. It is summer and time to get a bikini and go swimming. We have seen one article from 62 total with the word bikini, so we clicked on it and ended up on

Instagram. The hypothesis is that we should see more similar articles in the next few days. In a couple of days, we have seen an increase of articles with bag of words bikini, swimsuit, braless, pantless, topless, nude, underwear, etc., content. The more we click, the more articles we will get.

Date	SUM -Bag of words	Total news	Proportion
7/1/2022	1	62	0.016129
7/2/2022	2	64	0.03125
...	...	...	...
7/30/2022	14	63	0.2222222
7/31/2022	20	64	0.3125

Table 5. Provides evidence of Facebook's recommendation engine algorithm and its behavior: source, the author.

Figure 1. The time series of the articles increase over the time of 31 days for Topic bikini: source author.

Is this difference and increase in proportion statistically significant? R is our friend (Jim, 2022). The best is to use R.

R Script	res1 <- prop.test(x = c(62, 1), n = c(64, 20)) => difference H0:po ≤ pe => 0.3125 ≤ 0.016 (H0 – null hypothesis) HA:po > pe (greater) 0.3125 > 0.016 (HA – an alternative hypothesis) res2 <- prop.test(x = c(62, 1), n = c(64, 20), alternative = "greater") => increase
Results	res1 ... res2 2-sample test for equality of proportions with continuity correction data: c(62, 1) out of c(64, 20) X-squared = 63.788, df = 1, p-value = 6.93e-16

	alternative hypothesis: greater 95 percent confidence interval: 0.7981568 1.0000000 sample estimates: prop 1 prop 2 0.96875 0.05000
The result's interpretation	The test's p-value is 6.93e-16, which is less than the alpha = 0.05 significance level. With a p-value of 6.93e-16, we may conclude that the proportion of bikinis has significantly increased. The result was statistically significant on a 95% level with a CI (confidence interval) CI=(0.781, 1.000).

Table 6. Provides related statistics: source, the author.

Conclusion Recommendation engines:

As we can see from the experiment, after 31 days, the number of articles regarding beautiful females has increased from 1.6% to 31.25%. The recommendation engine does its work and delivers articles per our request. The more we click, the more similar articles we will see. The objective is to maximize the time on the platform so we can be served more and more advertisements. The quality of the articles is entirely irrelevant. Sure we could say that this way recommendation engine is responsible for the polarization of society depending on the subject.

Conclusion Cambridge Analytica:

As we can see from the data, Cambridge Analytica (Merrill, 2022) was able to influence a pool of ~383k users. If we calculate a very favorable conversion rate of 25%, we could get 95.75k users joining the "Leave EU" camp due to Cambridge Analytica's involvement. Very low number. The primary issue is that "Remain in EU" had only 42% of "Leave EU" funds.

Results and Discussion

This section sums up the results and continues with a discussion.

Recommendation engines:

The paper talks about the exploration of the weaknesses in Facebook's algorithm. From the straightforward experiment, it is clear that the more we click on a particular subject, the more articles we will see. The recommendation engine does a perfect job of pleasing us. We confirm our interest by clicking on the article and giving the engine the green light to serve similar content. The experiment confirmed our suspicion that

Facebook's recommendation engine could be part of the polarization of society. What are the solutions?

The solution could be to modify recommendation engines to serve an antagonistic point of view and the whole spectrum. This is, unfortunately, unrealistic. Facebook's objective is to make money.

Cambridge Analytica:

As we can see from the data, Cambridge Analytica's influence on Brexit was overrated. The primary issue is that "Remain in EU" was heavily underfunded.

Conclusion

This section covers the most critical points of the study.

Conclusion Recommendation engines:

Conclusion:	There is strong evidence that Facebook's recommendation engine is working well. • It increased the number of articles from 1.6% to 31.25% in 31 days. • The result was statistically significant on a 95% level with a CI (confidence interval) CI=(0.781, 1.000).

Recommendation:	How to fix Facebook: • Modify recommendation engines to serve an antagonistic point of view and the whole spectrum. • Separate freedom of speech from freedom to publish articles to millions of users. • Users will have to publish the rating of the article. • The user has to be an expert in the field to be able to publish to the large population • Influencers would have to hire a PR firm to quarantine the quality of the articles

Table 7. Provides final conclusions: source, the author.

Conclusion Cambridge Analytica:

As we can see from the data, **Cambridge Analytica's influence on Brexit was overrated**. Cambridge Analytica could convert approximately ~95.75k users (25% conversion rate) from 17,410,742 to Leave EU = 0.54%. The result from the PERT model, where the conversion rate is 9.3%, gave us ~35k users => 0.2% from 17,410,742 to Leave EU.

References and bibliography

Citation of websites

1. AVOCADO, A. (2020, December 18). The Latest UK Social Media Statistics for 2016. Avocado Social. https://www.avocadosocial.com/the-latest-uk-social-media-statistics-for-2016/
2. BBC. (2016, June 24). EU Referendum Results. BBC News. https://www.bbc.co.uk/news/politics/eu_referendum/results
3. Bell, M. (2022, July 14). A Three-Point Estimating Technique: PERT. Project Management Academy Resources. https://projectmanagementacademy.net/resources/blog/a-three-point-estimating-technique-pert/
4. British Council. (n.d.). The rise of fake news. LearnEnglish Teens - British Council. https://learnenglishteens.britishcouncil.org/skills/reading/c1-reading/rise-fake-news
5. Duffield, C. (2021, June 22). When was the Brexit vote? Timeline of the UK's departure from the EU 5 years on from the referendum. Inews.Co.Uk. https://inews.co.uk/news/when-was-the-brexit-vote-

timeline-of-the-uks-departure-from-the-eu-5-years-on-from-the-referendum-1065398

6. Franek, K. (2021, April 4). How Facebook Makes Money: Business Model Explained. KAMIL FRANEK | Business Analytics. https://www.kamilfranek.com/how-facebook-makes-money-business-model-explained/
7. Fiegerman, S. (2017, February 1). Facebook is closing in on 2 billion users. CNNMoney. https://money.cnn.com/2017/02/01/technology/facebook-earnings/index.html
8. Grimaldi, TJ (2022, March 21). If Facebook Removes Your Post, Is It Violating Your Freedom of Speech? TJ Grimaldi. https://www.tjgrimaldi.com/facebook-freedom-of-speech/
9. Investopedia. (2022, April 28). Investopedia. https://www.investopedia.com/ask/answers/120114/how-does-twitter-twtr-make-money.asp
10. Jim. (2022, May 28). Two Sample Proportions test in R-Complete Guide. R-Bloggers. https://www.r-bloggers.com/2022/05/two-sample-proportions-test-in-r-complete-guide/

11. KEMP, S. (2022, January 8). The Latest Facebook Statistics: Everything You Need to Know. DataReportal – Global Digital Insights. https://datareportal.com/essential-facebook-stats
12. Laterza, V. (2021, March 1). Could Cambridge Analytica Have Delivered Donald Trump's 2016 Presidential Victory? An Anthropologist's Look at Big Data and Political Campaigning. Public Anthropologist. https://brill.com/view/journals/puan/3/1/article-p119_119.xml?language=en
13. Leonard, K. (2022, May 27). 6 Different Ways Google Makes Money. SeekingAlpha. https://seekingalpha.com/article/4469984-how-does-google-make-money
14. Mailchimp (n.d.). Email Marketing Benchmarks and Statistics by Industry.. https://mailchimp.com/resources/email-marketing-benchmarks/
15. Martin, D. (2018, March 21). Facebook data scandal: What you need to know. DW.COM. https://www.dw.com/en/facebooks-cambridge-analytica-data-scandal-what-you-need-to-know/a-43071390
16. Martin, D. (2018a, March 27). What role did Cambridge Analytica play in the Brexit vote? DW.COM. https://www.dw.com/en/what-role-did-cambridge-analytica-play-in-the-brexit-vote/a-43151460

17. Merrill, J. (2022, July 21). Cambridge Analytica used these 5 political ads to target voters. Quartz. https://qz.com/1782348/cambridge-analytica-used-these-5-political-ads-to-target-voters/

18. OECD. (2022, March 1). Disentangling untruths online: Creators, spreaders and how to stop them. OECD. https://goingdigital.oecd.org/data/notes/No23_ToolkitNote_UntruthsOnline.pdf

19. RPubs - Text Analysis using SVM. (2019, September 30). RPubs. https://rpubs.com/masmit11/533879

20. Scribbr. (2022, July 6th). Free APA Citation Generator | Verified by Experts. Scribbr. https://www.scribbr.com/apa-citation-generator/new/webpage/

21. Staiger, U. (2016, June 16). Undecided on the EU referendum? These are the three questions to ask yourself. The Conversation. https://theconversation.com/undecided-on-the-eu-referendum-these-are-the-three-questions-to-ask-yourself-61099

22. Statista. (2021, February 11). EU referendum campaign groups' advertising spend in the United Kingdom (UK) 2016. https://www.statista.com/statistics/1031993/eu-referendum-campaign-groups-advertising-spend-in-the-uk/

23. Statista. (2022, July 7). UK: Facebook users 2018–2022. https://www.statista.com/statistics/1012080/uk-monthly-numbers-facebook-users/

24. UN (2019, January 23). UN News. https://news.un.org/en/story/2019/01/1030802

25. Usg. (n.d.). Usg. https://www.usg.edu/galileo/skills/unit07/internet07_02.phtml

26. Viktor (2022, June 17). What Happened To Myspace? Why Did It Fail? Productmint. https://productmint.com/what-happened-to-myspace/

27. Vile, J. (2009, January 1). False Speech. The First Amendment Encyclopedia. https://www.mtsu.edu/first-amendment/article/1506/false-speech

28. Wikipedia. (2021a, July 8). Absolute truth. Simple English Wikipedia, the Free Encyclopedia. https://simple.wikipedia.org/wiki/Absolute_truth

29. Wikipedia. (2022a, June 28). Friendster. Wikipedia. https://en.wikipedia.org/wiki/Friendster

30. Wikipedia. (2022b, July 27). JEL classification codes. Wikipedia. https://en.wikipedia.org/wiki/JEL_classification_codes

31. Wikipedia. (2022c, July 31). Meta Platforms. Wikipedia. https://en.wikipedia.org/wiki/Meta_Platforms

32. Wikipedia. (2022d, August 2). Google. Wikipedia. https://en.wikipedia.org/wiki/Google

33. Wikipedia. (2022e, July 26). Facebook–Cambridge Analytica data scandal. Wikipedia. https://en.wikipedia.org/wiki/Facebook%E2%80%93Cambridge_Analytica_data_scandal

34. Wright, G. (2021, November 1). ARPANET. SearchNetworking. https://www.techtarget.com/searchnetworking/definition/ARPANET

Contact information

Name of the author: Jiri Medlen

Affiliation (University): LIGS University student

Email: jiri.medlen@gmail.com

Contact information

Name of the author: Patrick Medlen

Affiliation (University): California State University, Fullerton

Email: pmedlen1@gmail.com

Did Fake News on Facebook Influence Electoral and Health Decisions?

Laura A. McCoy

Abstract

This paper reviews literature and research revolving around the issue of Fake News and Facebook's response to it around the 2016 and 2020 United States presidential elections and posted Fake News regarding Covid 19 in 2020 and 2021. The objective is to show the presence of Fake News on Facebook and explore the question of whether Facebook's policies and practices exaggerate the presence and circulation of Fake News. The settings of Facebook's algorithms are set to allow social information to flow on the social media platform. Evidence does not suggest Facebook practices are set for spread of false information only. They are set to be a social sharing site.

Keywords: *Facebook, Facebook Algorithms, Fake News, Social Media*

JEL Classification: *C8, D7, L1, L2, O3, Z1*

Introduction

Fake news was rumored in connection with the 2016 United States presidential election. Everywhere was a buzz during the 2020 Election. There were also constant droppings of news on the world-wide pandemic. It was rumored as false. In surprising action, Facebook allowed research by dual universities in the United States and France. The study progressed to the point of being peer reviewed. Facebook ended the study before it was published. The looming question was "did Facebook set in motion the process to reward fake news?"

The Spread of Fake News

Ben Gilbert in *Business Insider* November 6, 2019, reported that Facebook is the largest platform on social media. They claim two billion site users. The concept of watching over what is posted on the site seems overwhelming. Oversight was not always in the forefront. It was rumored misleading postings on Facebook affected the 2016 United States election between candidates Hillary Clinton and Donald Trump.

Yet the issue did not move into mainstream concern until the 2020 re-election of Donald Trump and challenger Joe Biden approached. As the election heated up in 2019, Facebook data captured a hundred fake news stories. And the surprising aspect was the view count of 150 million.

An example of a false story that appeared during the 2020 election period was that Trump's grandfather was a KKK member, did not pay taxes and worked as a pimp.

The complex task of monitoring Facebook posts was exacerbated in 2020 with the worldwide pandemic and the explosion of information in the public arena.

Facebook allows researchers access to its user data

Earlier in May 2019, Heidi Ledford posted in *Nature.com* that it was a shocking move when Facebook gave a research team its raw data. The team was looking at deciding if Facebook facilitated the spread of false information.

The study reached several conclusions:

1. Everyone can see clearly that something is true, but it can be hard to scientifically prove.
2. They believed Facebook did have processes in place to protect the right to one's ability to express themselves.

3. It was determined Facebook did have systems in place to identify and delete fake news.
4. The researchers established a pattern of false data moving from Facebook to Twitter and then being reposted to Facebook.
5. The researchers believed the fake information did influence human behavior and therefore influenced the elections.
6. Evidence established fast information was clicked on six times as often as facts during the period of the 2020 election.

In March 2020, Mark Travers reviewed in Forbes the spread of fake news on Facebook. Facebook is largely considered a social media site. The graph highlights the level of untrustworthy news sources on various social media sites.

Figure 1.

Untrustworthy news websites and other sources

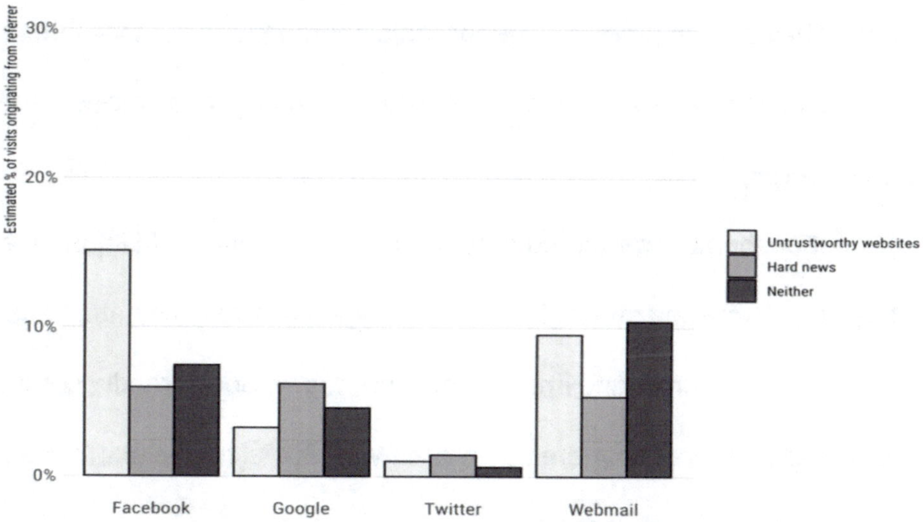

Source. Guess “et al.”, 2020

What was not studied in this research was the affect the fake data had on viewers. It could be proven that fake news was posted. But it is unable to prove that fake data changed opinions. And did not address change in viewers actions.

Researchers suggested it is hard to change a voter’s mind. Voters, including older voters, sought fake news on untrustworthy sights. Readers stayed longer on fake sites than accepted news sites. The report clearly noted Face book did remove many unverified entries and videos.

Fear and Anger fuel Fake news

Rachel Gilmore of *Global News* reported on May 19, 2021, that Facebook and Instagram had 18 million fake Covid news entries taken down. They did not pinpoint a geographic source location. It was stressed fake news can be generated and forwarded with negative emotion such as fear or anger.

Facebook commented that nothing users post could injure users. They also discussed strategies to encourage users to vaccinate. Facebook reports they will grow and improve as a company. Social media companies want user attention, so more ads are viewed. Social media platforms make their income with paid advertising.

The question persisted. Did Facebook set their systems to perpetuate fake news.

The response continues to reflect: Social platforms are set up to allow any user to post, share and like posts. Social Media does not require facts be posted or check to see posts are facts. Users can post information that is not true. This occurs as jokes between friends and is common among different supporters in political elections.

While Covid was in progress users posted information and videos. They claimed to be professionals. The information was copied and shared by users during the panic of the pandemic. They may have seen value in the information shared. It was known the data was not fact checked but the information was posted and shared and treated as factual.

The early days of the pandemic was a time greatly lacking in facts from experts such as the World Health Organization and the Center for Disease Control. People spoke firmly as if opinion was fact. Individuals were reported as very sick and dying horrible deaths. No treatment or cure was known. Individuals argued for hours over divisive issues such as wearing masks. The worldwide pandemic was a scary time.

Did Facebook Speed the Spread of Fake News?

Research aimed to prove Facebooks algorithms sped the spread of fake news was reported in the Washington Post on September 3, 2021. The study covered August 2020 though January 2021. It was a combined study between New York University (Tandon School of Engineering) and the Université Grenoble Alpes in France. The study progressed to the point of being peer reviewed.

The study found that fake news had six times more actions including likes, comments, and shares than those that post verified news. Examples of verified news include CNN and in the health setting the Center for Disease Control. This study was a very unusual method to scientifically document the processing of fake news on a social media site. They attempted to prove that Facebook set up to reward those that post fake news. That Facebook algorithms favor bias on one side of the political side or the other. This was an accusation that prompted the study.

Before publication, Facebook discontinued the professors' contract to study information on Facebook. The professors involved were Damon McCoy, a computer science and engineering professor, and Laura Edelson, a researcher and Ph.D. Candidate. In dissolving the contract Facebook claimed collecting data for the study was in violation of "2019 U.S. Federal Trade Commission privacy settlement." Per the agreement being involved in the study was on a volunteer basis. The data was collected via a downloaded widget.

The researcher Edelson commented to the Washington Post: The study did not demonstrate Facebook manipulating bias. It was noted the Right has more information labeled as fake news. False information does increase user interest. Facebook system did spread fake news but that is the nature of a social media site. Individual users can post, and other users can react to or share the information. Facebook is an efficient social media site and therefore fake information spread especially smoothly.

The next day, September 4, 2021, Elizabeth Dwoskin of the Washington Post released more information on the fake news story. Fake news became a concern in 2016. It was suspected that fake news affected the 2016 United States Election. The rumor floated that Facebook spread the false news and rewarded those that posted on the site. It was implied that users wanted more fake news and responded to what was posted.

Rebekah Tromble, director of the Institute for Data, Democracy and Politics at George Washington University, reviewed the study's findings. She found the NYU study was well designed covered the issues to be studied well.

Facebook did respond that the NYU research did uncover that users did seem interested and became engaged with fake news. Facebook notes those that saw or read the posts were not counted. (Facebook does not give out viewer counts.) Facebook stresses they do fact check posts in 60 languages. They claim to remove posts as they see fit.

It is questioned how Facebook decides on information to remove. There is no documentation for damage fake information caused. Facebook tightly controls its data and access is not allowed.

The Washington Post noted fake news was spread during the Covid pandemic. Even President Biden commented Fake health news could hurt people. The White House says they asked for Covid data from Facebook and the request has not been filled. Some believe users on Facebook express being more anti treatment and vaccination than the mainstream media news. Users on Facebook have even denied the existence of the pandemic.

Facebook ended the Fake news study citing the violation of user privacy. The 2019 U.S. Federal Trade Commission did comment there is a process for research. The question of why Facebook shut down the study is in question. What are they trying to hide?

"Edelson said the study showed that Facebook algorithms were not rewarding partisanship or bias or favoring sites on one side of the political spectrum, as some critics have claimed. She said that Facebook amplifies misinformation because it does well with users, and the sites that happen to have more misinformation are on the right. Among publishers categorized as on the far right, those that share misinformation get a majority — or 68 percent — of all engagement from users. (Dwoskin, 2021)"

Why We Don't Click

The NYU study did not research users that didn't click on topics because Facebook did not release that data to the researchers. In October 2020 a group of researchers posted in Journal of Computer-Mediated

Communication, a well-researched study of social media addressing why we don't click.

One point was individuals active on social media feel a sense of social connection. They feel better about themselves. Individual just looking at social media feed can compare themselves to the happy life of the poster and feel very bad about themselves. The chart gives an example of the types of clickers studied.

Figure 2.

Social Media Use Conceptual Categories

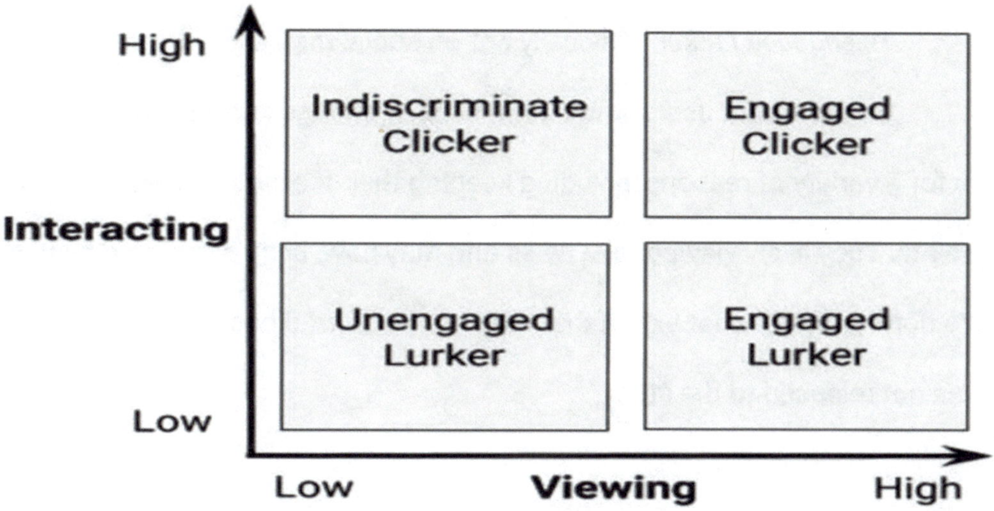

Source. Ellison "at el.", 2020

Indiscriminate Clicker - Some users simply slide through the feed and click with no seeming reason.

Engaged Clicker - These follow others closely and offer feedback on posts often expressing joy.

Engaged Lurker - Some users stay quiet and do not respond to others. They may feel this allows privacy. They may respond in other ways. Such as one on one private channels. They may be looking for information on others. One commented that he did not respond to a girl in a swimsuit because he figured she did not post it for him. They may fear their feed being changed by clicking. Or any response.

Unengaged Lurker - Basically not on social media.

Social media users who do not click or engage in social media do so for a variety of reasons including keeping their feelings and expressions private. They likely viewed fake news and may have been influenced by it. We don't know to what extent that may have occurred because the data was not released to the study.

Fear runs rampant

Fake news was rumored during the 2016 United States election. By the 2020 presidential election the planet was emersed in a worldwide pandemic. Little was officially released by the accepted experts and very little of that was believed by the public. People were said to be dying horrible deaths, but little looked different to most of the public. The locked-down public had social media, including Facebook, as one of its few release valve points and they used it. As usual political candidates were muddied with partial and complete untruths. Did this affect the election results? Although the public can suspect that it did, science to this point has not proven the election results were affected.

Fueled by fear and anger social media users asked each other if they knew anyone that was actually sick. Government conspiracy questions were raised and discussed actively on Facebook. "Was the Pandemic just a made-up excuse to lock us down and close our businesses?" Not surprisingly, people panicked. Runs were made on supplies and shortages from food to toilet paper arose. People who normally fed their families were out of work and hungry. Food banks were called on to feed extreme numbers.

"Why were we actually locked in our homes? Were we being told we were being vaccinated against the virus when something far more sinister was being injected into our bodies?" Experts appeared out of nowhere. In

Facebook videos, they offered theories on the virus. They claimed to believe what they offered but at that point in time no verification was available. Later those claiming to be medical professionals offered video theories of successful lifesaving treatment of their patients. Again, verification was not available at that point in time.

Facebook took down the "popup" opinions almost as quickly as they were posted. Those sharing the opinions began leading the "share" with a statement of "watch this quickly before it is censored." Many may have viewed posted official announcements and the opinions. For many reasons, including fear, they did not choose to click or comment. Again, Facebook did not release the counts on this data. Officials were moving at record speed to pull together vaccinations. A process that is normally safety checked over years was streamlined to months.

Conclusion

This paper reviews literature and research revolving around the issue of Fake News and Facebook's response to it around the 2016 and 2020 United States presidential elections and posted Fake News regarding Covid 19 in 2020 and 2021. Did this affect the election results? Although the public can suspect that it did, science to this point has not proven the election results were affected. Many may have viewed posted official announcements and the opinions. For many reasons, including fear, they did not choose to click or comment. Facebook did not release the counts on this data.

Fake News was clearly present on Facebook but there is little to support that Facebook's policies and practices exaggerate the presence and circulation of Fake News. The settings of Facebook's algorithms are set to allow social information to flow on the social media platform. Evidence does not suggest Facebook practices are set for spread of false information only. They are set to be a social sharing site.

References

Dwoskin, Elizabeth. "Misinformation on Facebook Got Six Times More Clicks than Factual News during the 2020 Election, Study Says." Washington Post, 4 Sept. 2021, www.washingtonpost.com/technology/2021/09/03/facebook-misinformation-nyu-study/.

Ellison, N, et al. "Journal of Computer-Mediated Communication,." Journal of Computer-Mediated Communication, vol. 25, no. 6, 2020, pp. 402–426, 10.1093/jcmc/zmaa013.

Gilbert, Ben. "The 10 Most-Viewed Fake-News Stories on Facebook in 2019 Were Just Revealed in a New Report." Business Insider, 6 Nov. 2019, www.businessinsider.com/most-viewed-fake-news-stories-shared-on-facebook-2019-2019-11.

Gilmore, Rachel. "Fake News on Facebook: 18 Million Posts Containing COVID-19 Misinformation Removed - National | Globalnews.ca." Global News, 19 May 2021, globalnews.ca/news/7876321/covid-19-misinformation-social-media-facebook-instagram/.

Ledford, Heidi. "Facebook Gives Social Scientists Unprecedented Access to Its User Data." Nature, vol. 41586-019-01447, no. 5, 3 May 2019, 10.1038/d41586-019-01447-5. Accessed 28 Aug. 2019.

The Washington Post. "Misinformation on Facebook Got Six Times More Clicks than Factual News during the 2020 Election, Study Says | NYU Tandon School of Engineering." Engineering.nyu.edu, 2021, engineering.nyu.edu/news/misinformation-facebook-got-six-times-more-clicks-factual-news-during-2020-election-study-says.

Travers, Mark. "Facebook Spreads Fake News Faster than Any Other Social Website, according to New Research." Forbes, 2020, www.forbes.com/sites/traversmark/2020/03/21/facebook-spreads-fake-news-faster-than-any-other-social-website-according-to-new-research/?sh=72a97e106e1a. Accessed 4 Sept. 2022.

Contact information
Name of the author: Laura A. McCoy
Affiliation (University): LIGS University student
Email: lmccy@wcc.net

The Art of Fake News Creation and Dissemination

Jiri Medlen, Patrick Medlen

Abstract

The study aimed to analyze the art of "fake news" and its creation and dissemination. Creating high-quality fake news and spreading it with low detection is complex and requires considerable effort. We examined the definition of fake news, its history, and what influences its spread. We studied several examples to understand the different types of fake news and analyzed Social Media platforms' news dissemination. Additionally, we looked at the first amendment's role in protecting fake news and the design and implementation of news-farms using the Twitter platform and Twitter API, which individuals and various entities can use for marketing purposes and the distribution of fake news. Finally, we investigated financial market manipulation, a pump-and-dump technique used to manipulate GME stock, and Elon Musk's cryptocurrency manipulation.

Keywords: *Facebook, Meta, sentiment, social media, Twitter*

JEL Classification: *C10, C12, C90, D12*

Introduction

Is fake news a phenomenon of modern society, or is it as old as human history? According to a Cambridge academic, the 3000-year-old story of Noah's Ark is an early example of fake news (Worthington, 2019). The claim that Jesus married Mary Magdalene is another example of fake news (Kruger, 2017). Lastly, Pope Francis claimed that the first case of misinformation is in the Bible, the serpent's message of temptation, and that it was humanity's 'first fake news' occurrence (BBC, 2018).

Is fake news the only invention, or have we pushed the envelope further? One example is Grigori Potëmkin, who built fake villages along the road where Catherine the Great traveled (Merriam-Webster Dictionary, 2022). Czechoslovakian intelligence agencies used the same technique in the 1950s, creating fake Austrian villages for people trying to escape communism. They celebrated after escaping, but in the morning, they realized they were still in Czechoslovakia, after which the escapees promptly got arrested.

As for fake news' role in communist countries, because they could not compete economically, they generated fake news (forming public opinion sounds better) and support for minorities or any moment thinkable in the west to destabilize the west through divide and conquer strategies.

Concerning examples of this in modern times, is social media to blame for such rapid dissemination? To better answer this question, a brief overview of the Internet's history will prove helpful. The Internet is one of the most substantial developments in this century as it wholly democratized knowledge and created the powerful opportunity of selling and publishing, although, unfortunately, selling and publishing rights shifted from a few privileged individuals to everyone.

The Internet's origins began with ARPANET (The U.S. Advanced Research Projects Agency Network) in 1968 (Wright, 2021). Universities primarily used ARPANET for research purposes, and it was the Internet's predecessor, although, at that time, the communication protocols were weak and not standardized. However, a breakthrough came with the invention of TCP/IP (Transfer Control Protocol/Internetwork Protocol), and as ARPANET switched to TCP/IP on January 1st, 1983, it is considered the official birthday of the Internet (Usg, n.d.).

The beginning was hard. We could handle mostly text with Gopher and file transfer with FTP (File Transfer Protocol). To connect to the server, Telnet was and still is a must. The email significantly improved, and we could use Usenet newsgroups (moderated). IRC (Internet Relay Chat) was another outstanding achievement. The real change came with Hypertext transfer protocol – a.k.a. "The Web" and Netscape's browser, which could handle images. The additional improvement came from a Uniform Resource Locator (URL) for the servers. However, it is hard for humans to remember numbers like http://198.15.93.98 better would be a text, and another invention solved that. The Domain Name System (DNS) turns domain names into IP addresses.

How do you find the servers? The following invention came quickly, and the answer was directory Yahoo. It was better but not great. Search engines (Infoseek, Alta Vista, and later Google (Wikipedia, 2022d)) started to pop up. The next significant milestone was online shopping, and eBay and later Amazon was born.

Innovation riched Social Media space, and Myspace started in 2003, and Friendster started in 2002 (Wikipedia, 2022a) were created (Viktor, 2022). This started the Social Media (SM) revolution. The biggest name in the SM space today is Facebook (FB) (today Meta), and FB started in 2004 (Wikipedia, 2022c). Let us look at the most prominent names, Google, Twitter, and Facebook.

How is Google making money? Google revolutionized the advertisement space (Leonard, 2022), and most of the revenue is from Google Ads. Google is a search engine so that users will perform a search, review results quickly, and move on with the task. Google does not own the content. It will index whatever web server has. Good or bad, true or false, is entirely irrelevant for Google.

How does Twitter make money? Twitter makes money from advertisements and data selling (Investopedia, 2022).

How does Facebook make money? Most of the revenue is from Facebook and Instagram apps (Franek, 2021). Unlike with Google, users publish on Facebook's platform; in some sense, Facebook can monitor the content if required. At this point, Facebook is operating under the belief that people are good and they would self-monitor themselves and publish high-quality documents. So it is the end user's responsibility. This is a naive premise. Today platforms like Facebook and Twitter give ordinary people the power, ability, and the freedom to publish. With freedom comes big responsibility. People should publish only true and quality posts. Only experts should give, e.g., medical advice, but that is no longer the case, as anyone can talk about anything, and social media is a cesspool.

Can Facebook or Twitter remove any posts, and by doing it, is Facebook or Twitter violating the First Amendment? The First Amendment protects free speech in public property or forums that the public or government owes. Facebook is a private company that can remove posts that are not written according to its published guidelines (Grimaldi, 2022).

Does the First Amendment protect false statements? The First Amendment's purpose is to further the pursuit of truth; therefore, untruth is not protected (Vile, 2009). However, sometimes it might be impossible to distinguish truth from untruths, so untruths may sometimes be unpunished. Why is it so hard to find the truth? Let us look at the absolute truth. Does it exist? One example of absolute truth is no round squares (Wikipedia, 2021a). Let us try other examples.

A religious person would claim that God exists.

The atheist would claim that God does not exist.

Who is right?

Wine is good for you.

Wine is bad for you.

Who is right?

Vaccination is good for you.

Vaccination is bad for you.

Who is right?

Why is it so hard to monitor the quality of the posts (OECD, 2022), and why Twitter and Facebook cannot remove them so easily? How can we detect fake news using machine learning (ML)? ML could help. However, it requires supervised learning and, therefore, manual labeling. The main issue is that the labeling team might sometimes have difficulty distinguishing between fake news and what is not. After we have enough examples, we could use, e.g., Naïve Bayes or SVM for the modeling (training and testing with a typical split of 70/30 or 80/20). We used Python and Anaconda distribution 3.7. Another great possibility is to use R (RPubs - Text Analysis using SVM, 2019) or RapidMiner (great for non-programmers with drag&drop functionality). We used classification, and it is 2 class problem (Fake post-YES/NO). The basic idea is straightforward. Some words will be more prominent for each class.

Well. How about other examples?

Post	Fake post YES/NO	Notes

I saw Jesus walking on the Golden gate bridge.	YES	The probability of this event is very low => most likely fake news
The mortality rate of COVID-19 Omicron variant BA.5 is increasing.	?	This is hard to tell – only the author can tell for sure.
Pelosi's Plane Lands in Taiwan Despite China Warning.	NO	

Table 1. Provides examples of some hypothetical posts: source, the author.

Why are people writing fake news? What is their motivation (British Council, n.d.).)?

4. Feed the ego. The author thinks he/she is brighter than the rest of us.

5. Politically motivated. He/she is trying to incriminate opponents. Alternatively, simply divide and conquer the society. Russia and China are manipulating elections in the US.
6. Simply for a profit.

What is selling more fear versus non-fear news?

Unfortunately, the latest research confirms that fear is the best-selling brand today. It is probably still because of our survival instinct (UN, 2019).

Facebook and Twitter are making money from advertisements, and their main objective is to try to please the users and tell them what they want to hear so they stay on the platform as long as possible so FB and Twitter can to serve them more and more adds. The basic technology they are using is the Recommendation engines.

What about today's examples of fake news? We will get to it.

Material and Methods

This section covers the used methods and methodology.

Material:

We installed Python Anaconda 3.7 distribution. Twitter API (Twitter Docs, 2022) library Twython (McGrath, 2022) or Tweepy (Tweepy Docs, 2022). For Sentiment analysis Textblob (Loria, 2022).

Methods:

- Design and implementation of news-farms using the Twitter platform and Twitter API using Python and Twython library.
- Review articles regarding the pump-and-dump technique used to manipulate the stock.
- Review articles regarding Elon's crypto manipulation.

Model and Data

This section covers the used models, collected data, and strategy for collecting Tweets.

Literature review – Twython (Twitter API)

As we can see, Russia and China are merrily using our platforms like Facebook and Twitter to form (manipulate) public opinion on their strategic interests. How can this be done? How many accounts would we need to move the needle? How to avoid detection?

The first question is, what is the objective of the manipulation? Do we need perfect English or not? Let us assume we would like perfect English. Typically Russians would indirectly hire students from the US with the task of writing targeted articles. The task can be a new article or simply a reply to a Blog. The objective is to contradict something and use a simple internal division in the country (divide and conquer) model. If it is not a blog, We have to do **seeding** of the article, create multiple websites, host the articles there and link them. It takes time to establish a presence on the web and, depending on the budget, start Search Engine Optimization (SEO) to get organic traffic. With more money, it would be possible to purchase some Google Ads (Google Ads, 2022).

Additionally, it might be a good idea to establish some Facebook pages and link them with the websites. Great start. What else can be done? Next, it is essential to establish Twitter accounts. To be able to make a difference, we would need min 100k accounts or more. For that, we could use automation such as Selenium (manually doing it would be very time-consuming). We could use one Gmail account, but the detection would be simple with a simple SQL query. So we need more Gmail accounts as well, so we need more automation. We have another problem all accounts are using the same IP address. Detection is simple with a simple SQL query. To combat that, we need to add IP rotation and associate the IP address with the account.

Let us start with 100 Twitter accounts. Just preparing and creating 100 Twitter accounts is lots of work, but we can do it manually at this point. Knowing all the steps is essential before investing in automation (lots of work - AIP is always the preferable method before Selenium). Now it is time to start with Twitter API. Twitter is using OAUTH_TOKEN, so for each account, we needed

IP address + Gmail + OAUTH_TOKEN examples only:

#APP_KEY = "etRmOPenBOeUereHOPed"

#APP_SECRET = "zH4lGteUweRTSfHI19OPtJeO4FBeEs23kScU2erUwl"

#OAUTH_TOKEN = "1959705427e4w4tuGrTSeH24AWtW8eYirUEIDSfRTolOnftof"

#OAUTH_TOKEN_SECRET ="RTDur33eyyyE22odwWgfeudDewOfsfdU3rrtToS"

We need to link accounts and follow each other (not all of them link to each other). Now we have accounts, but nobody knows about them (they are a top secret at this point). The best start is to explore Query API and start Twitter monitoring.

twitter = Twython(Token['APP_KEY'], Token['APP_SECRET'], Token['OAUTH_TOKEN'], Token['OAUTH_TOKEN_SECRET'])

Search something interesting in variable q=item. We are using 'extended' mode.

search_results = twitter.search(q=item, count=100, tweet_mode='extended').

The query has a limit to we rotate accounts + IP addresses, of course.

We had to make sure all accounts were working before following each other. Now it was important to establish the present. The best is to look at trends and establish a strategy for re-tweet (Ria, 2014).

dailyTrend = twitter.getDailyTrends(); print (dailyTrend) # Daily Trend

weeklyTrend = twitter.getWeeklyTrends(); print (weeklyTrend) # Weekly Trend

twitter.retweet(id = "TWEET_ID") # re-tweet

Why is re-tweet important? We want others to follow our accounts. It takes some time to establish presents on the web. Creating a boot and re-tweet based on search queries or trends is entirely possible (Ria, 2014). Why re-tweet? To increase the probability that others would follow (Pick, 2020). After some time, it is possible to start the process of **disseminating** own tweets. Of course, keep creating more Twitter accounts, and do not forget Facebook, Google, and other SM.

Conclusion:

Creating and maintaining a quality news-farm is lots of work, and programming skill is required.

Literature review – Textblob:

Here we review Textblob and how to use it to extract sentiment. For the creation of a functional bot might be interesting to add sentiment analysis. Sentiment could be another dimension for deciding on what to re-tweet. Essentially we could construct a machine learning model to assess what is an excellent article to re-tweet.

```
analysis = TextBlob(clean_tweet(tweet)) # create TextBlob object of passed tweet text
# set sentiment
if analysis.sentiment.polarity > 0:
    return 'positive'
elif analysis.sentiment.polarity == 0:
    return 'neutral'
else:
    return 'negative'
```

Conclusion: With TextBlob, sentiment is simple. However, we might have to create our model to use sentiment towards some object, e.g., PayPal. Example: "I love tomatoes, I hate potatoes, and I will pay by PayPal." In this case, sentiment towards PayPal is neutral. Another example is: "Performance of company's ABC stock is poor." Is this negative sentiment? Sometimes it is tricky to define what sentiment is.

Literature review – the pump-and-dump technique used to manipulate GME:

The idea of using sentiment analysis is not new. In the year 2000, many startups popped up and started playing with the idea. Typically, we used yahoo finance (GME, 2022). Unfortunately, the correlation was weak, and market correction killed many companies based on the "new economy." However, GME and the year Jan 1st, 2021 changed it. Some companies abused the short selling of GME stock (Short Selling, 2022). Short selling is a high-risk investment and can lose more than the original investment. Keith Gill (Gill, 2022) discovered that many hedge funds are making lots of money by betting on GME. After his post under the username DeepFuckingValue (DFV) on Reddit (subreddit r/wallstreetbets) and Roaring Kitty on Twitter, the war started. As a result, by the end of January 2021, Melvin Capital lost 30 percent of its value, and the total damage for short sellers was ~$6 billion due to the squeeze. When the poor lose money, nobody cares. We need a Congressional hearing when the rich lose money (Wiki, 2022).

Conclusion: Our main objective was to build a platform that can be used for, e.g., analysis or GME stock manipulation if desired. Text mining of GME was done by Abhinav Anand (Abhinav, 2021), and they proved that there is a correlation between GME stock and messages on r/wallstreetbets exists.

Literature review – Elon's crypto manipulation:

In our following example, we looked at Elon's tweets and their correlation with crypto. Elon definitely does not need help from the news-farm. Let us zoom on Dogecoin (The Economic Times, 2022; Reuters, 2021). See Table 2 for details.

27 Jun, 2022, 03.17 PM IST	Dogecoin zooms 13% in a day and it's not just after Musk's push
05 Apr, 2022, 02.06 PM IST	Dogecoin up 40% in 3 weeks!
28 Mar, 2022, 04.16 PM IST	Elon Musk again sparks 10% rise in Dogecoin.

14 Jan, 2022, 02.45 PM IST	Elon Musk pumps Dogecoin with yet another tweet, token surges 25%

Table 2. Dogecoin tweets: source, the author.

Conclusion: Our second example shows social media's power and how simple it is to manipulate the market if you are Elon.

Results and Discussion

This section sums up the results and continues with a discussion. The paper's core is to build a news-farm platform that can be used for marketing or analyzing whatever the user needs from Twitter. However, it is lots of work and requires extensive programming experience to build one.

Today, the mini-platform is used for analysis only. The first GME example has shown the potential of such a platform for stock manipulation, thanks to Abhinav Anand's analysis. When analyzing microblogs and associated sentiment, we must learn the jargon and create new models. Textblob does not know how to interpret "tendies" or "gay bears" (Wiki, 2022a). The second example has shown the power of social media and how easy it is to manipulate the market if you are a powerful influencer. Even Elon must be careful. Elon Musk Sued for $258 Billion for influencing Doge.

Conclusion

This section covers the most critical points of the study.

Conclusion:	To manipulate a market if you are nobody is challenging and lots of work, but it can be done. It is a piece of cake if you are a significant influencer like Elon Musk, but even he has to be careful.
Recommendation:	100 accounts are suitable for analysis. However, 100k accounts would be needed to make a difference.

Table 3. Provides final conclusions: source, the author.

References and bibliography

Citation of websites

35. Abhinav, A. (2021, December 1). The Role of Reddit in the GameStop Short Squeeze. GameStop. https://www.iimb.ac.in/sites/default/files/2021-12/WP%20No.%20644.pdf
36. AVOCADO, A. (2020, December 18). The Latest UK Social Media Statistics for 2016. Avocado Social. https://www.avocadosocial.com/the-latest-uk-social-media-statistics-for-2016/
37. BBC. (2016, June 24). EU Referendum Results. BBC News. https://www.bbc.co.uk/news/politics/eu_referendum/results
38. BBC (2018, January 24). Pope says serpent temptation in Bible "first fake news." https://www.bbc.com/news/world-europe-42802295
39. Billio, M. (2021, October 7). GME: A Pump and Dump Scheme? GME. http://dspace.unive.it/handle/10579/19937
40. British Council. (n.d.). The rise of fake news. LearnEnglish Teens - British Council. https://learnenglishteens.britishcouncil.org/skills/reading/c1-reading/rise-fake-news

41. Bursztynsky, J. (2022, February 28). Google, Facebook work to stop spread of Russian anti-Ukraine disinformation with new changes. CNBC. https://www.cnbc.com/2022/02/28/google-facebook-battle-to-stop-spread-of-russian-disinformation.html
42. Franek, K. (2021, April 4). How Facebook Makes Money: Business Model Explained. KAMIL FRANEK | Business Analytics. https://www.kamilfranek.com/how-facebook-makes-money-business-model-explained/
43. Fiegerman, S. (2017, February 1). Facebook is closing in on 2 billion users. CNNMoney. https://money.cnn.com/2017/02/01/technology/facebook-earnings/index.html
44. GME. (2022, August 1). GME. https://finance.yahoo.com/quote/GME/
45. Gill, K (2022, August 9). Keith Gill. Wikipedia. https://en.wikipedia.org/wiki/Keith_Gill
46. Google Ads (2022, August 1). Google Ads. https://ads.google.com/intl/en_us/getstarted/
47. Grimaldi, TJ (2022, March 21). If Facebook Removes Your Post, Is It Violating Your Freedom of Speech? TJ Grimaldi. https://www.tjgrimaldi.com/facebook-freedom-of-speech/

48. Investopedia. (2022, April 28). Investopedia. https://www.investopedia.com/ask/answers/120114/how-does-twitter-twtr-make-money.asp

49. KEMP, S. (2022, January 8). The Latest Facebook Statistics: Everything You Need to Know. DataReportal – Global Digital Insights. https://datareportal.com/essential-facebook-stats

50. Kruger, M. J. (2017, October 31). 5 'Fake News' Stories People Believe About Early Christianity. The Gospel Coalition. https://www.thegospelcoalition.org/article/5-fake-news-stories-people-believe-about-early-christianity/

51. Leonard, K. (2022, May 27). 6 Different Ways Google Makes Money. SeekingAlpha. https://seekingalpha.com/article/4469984-how-does-google-make-money

52. Loria, S. (2022, August 1). TextBlob: Simplified Text Processing — TextBlob 0.16.0 documentation. TextBlob. https://textblob.readthedocs.io/en/dev/

53. Merriam-Webster Dictionary (2022, January 1). Potemkin village. https://www.merriam-webster.com/dictionary/Potemkin%20village

54. Mozur, P. (2021, December 2). Facebook and Twitter Remove Accounts Connected to China. The New York Times.

https://www.nytimes.com/2021/12/02/business/facebook-twitter-china-propaganda.html

55. OECD. (2022, March 1). Disentangling untruths online: Creators, spreaders and how to stop them. OECD. https://goingdigital.oecd.org/data/notes/No23_ToolkitNote_UntruthsOnline.pdf
56. Pick, T. (2020, March 28). 5 Great Reasons to Retweet Others on Twitter. B2B Marketing Blog | Webbiquity. https://webbiquity.com/social-media-marketing/5-great-reasons-to-retweet-others-on-twitter/
57. Reuters. (2021, November 9). How tweets by Tesla's Elon Musk have moved markets. The Economic Times. https://economictimes.indiatimes.com/markets/stocks/news/how-tweets-by-teslas-elon-musk-have-moved-markets/articleshow/87599113.cms
58. Ria, R. (2014, September 5). ReTweeting with your Twython Twitter Bot - Silkstream | Web Design Blog. Silkstream. https://www.silkstream.net/blog/2014/06/retweeting-with-your-twython-twitter-bot.html

59. Scribbr. (2022, July 6th). Free APA Citation Generator | Verified by Experts. Scribbr. https://www.scribbr.com/apa-citation-generator/new/webpage/

60. Short Selling. (2022, March 1). Investopedia. https://www.investopedia.com/terms/s/shortselling.asp

61. Team, O. M. (2022, June 17). Elon Musk Sued for $258 Billion For Influencing Dogecoin Price With Successive Tweets. Https://Www.Outlookindia.Com/. https://www.outlookindia.com/business/elon-musk-sued-for-258-billion-for-influencing-dogecoin-price-with-successive-tweets-news-202969

62. The Economic Times. (2022, August 16). https://economictimes.indiatimes.com/topic/elon-musk-tweet-about-baby-doge/news

63. Tweepy Docs. (2022, August 1). Tweepy. https://docs.tweepy.org/en/stable/

64. Twitter Docs. (2022, August 1). Docs | Twitter Developer Platform. https://developer.twitter.com/en/docs

65. UN (2019, January 23). UN News. https://news.un.org/en/story/2019/01/1030802

66. Usg. (n.d.). Usg. https://www.usg.edu/galileo/skills/unit07/internet07_02.phtml
67. Viktor (2022, June 17). What Happened To Myspace? Why Did It Fail? Productmint. https://productmint.com/what-happened-to-myspace/
68. Vile, J. (2009, January 1). False Speech. The First Amendment Encyclopedia. https://www.mtsu.edu/first-amendment/article/1506/false-speech
69. Wiki (2022, August 9). GameStop short squeeze. Wikipedia. https://en.wikipedia.org/wiki/GameStop_short_squeeze
70. Wiki (2022a, August 10). R/wallstreetbets. Wiki. https://en.wikipedia.org/wiki/R/wallstreetbets
71. Wikipedia. (2021a, July 8). Absolute truth. Simple English Wikipedia, the Free Encyclopedia. https://simple.wikipedia.org/wiki/Absolute_truth
72. Wikipedia. (2022a, June 28). Friendster. Wikipedia. https://en.wikipedia.org/wiki/Friendster
73. Wikipedia. (2022b, July 27). JEL classification codes. Wikipedia. https://en.wikipedia.org/wiki/JEL_classification_codes
74. Wikipedia. (2022c, July 31). Meta Platforms. Wikipedia. https://en.wikipedia.org/wiki/Meta_Platforms

75. Wikipedia. (2022d, August 2). Google. Wikipedia. https://en.wikipedia.org/wiki/Google

76. Wikipedia. (2022e, July 26). Facebook–Cambridge Analytica data scandal. Wikipedia. https://en.wikipedia.org/wiki/Facebook%E2%80%93Cambridge_Analytica_data_scandal

77. Worthington, M. (2019, November 26). 'Trickster god' used fake news in Babylonian Noah story. University of Cambridge. https://www.cam.ac.uk/research/news/trickster-god-used-fake-news-in-babylonian-noah-story

78. Wright, G. (2021, November 1). ARPANET. SearchNetworking. https://www.techtarget.com/searchnetworking/definition/ARPANET

Contact information

Name of the author: Patrick Medlen

Affiliation (University): California State University, Fullerton

Email: pmedlen1@gmail.com

Contact information

Name of the author: Jiri Medlen

Affiliation (University): LIGS University student

Email: jiri.medlen@gmail.com

Exploring Covid-19 Conspiracy Theories in Nigeria

Reuben Ufot Etuk

Abstract

The explosion of fake news in the forms of misinformation and conspiracy theories has become a serious threat to democracy and public trust. For instance, while the world was battling with the rapid spread of COVID-19 across nations, there was a parallel wide spread of information that make the general public to become suspicious of the circumstances surrounding the COVID-19 Pandemic. There were conspiracy theories suggesting intentional release of the COVID-19 virus for political and economic gains. The beliefs and spread of these conspiracy theories become so strong that the Director-general of the World Health Organization (WHO) warned that, we are not only fighting a pandemic, but also fighting an *infodemic*. This study therefore aims at exploring the conspiracy theories in the Nigerian context using mixed quantitative and qualitative methods. The findings reveal that respondents believe in conspiracy theories and the beliefs are based predominantly on two sources of information- social media and personal contacts. These beliefs lead to lack of trust in any preventive and control program, and even affected the vaccination rate significantly. The study further identify gap in public health communication as a key factor which allows the conspiracy theories to hold much grounds and thus suggests effective method for public communication to foster trusts for combating future outbreaks and pandemics.

Keywords: *Conspiracy theories, COVID-19, Disinformation, Fake news, Misinformation*.

JEL Classification: *I10, I12, I18*

Introduction

While the world was battling with the rapid spread of Corona Virus Disease (COVID-19) across nations, there was a parallel wide spread of conspiracy theories and misinformation that make the general public to become suspicious of the circumstances surrounding the COVID-19 Pandemic. The beliefs and spread of these conspiracy theories became so strong that the Director-general of the World Health Organization (WHO) warned that, we are not only fighting an epidemic, but also fighting an *infodemic* ...(WHO 2020). Conspiracy theories attempt to explain significant events and circumstances as the malevolent acts of secret and powerful groups (Douglas, K. M., 2021). Historically, all major events that took place in the past decades have always been faced with various conspiracy allegations that suggest an explanation involving plots hatched in secret by powerful group of persons. This also goes for major outbreaks of diseases. The Soviet union launched a misinformation campaign claiming that HIV was a biological weapon developed by the United States (Geissler E. & Sprinkle, R. H. 2013); and there was widespread belief that the HIV/AIDS as a conspiracy to kill Black people (Bogart & Thorburn, 2005; Bogart et al., 2010).). The Ebola outbreak in West Africa has its own dose of conspiracy theory, alleging the western world released it into West Africa (Abramowitz, S., McKune, S. L., Fallah, M. et al, 2017)

Immediately COVID-19 emerges, conspiracy theories were also released. Some people believed that COVID-19 was deliberately manufactured by the Chinese to wage war on the USA (or vice versa). As the pandemic progressed, others believed that COVID-19 was a hoax or was exaggerated by left-wingers as part of a plot to derail Donald Trump's reelection campaign (Douglas, K. M., 2021).

Nigerians were not left out in the conspiracy theories beliefs as illustrated in figure 1 below. At first many Nigerian citizens believed that COVID-19 is a "rich man's disease" as the media only report the death of rich and famous Nigerians from the disease. Some evangelicals claimed that the 5G network and the unavailable vaccines are tools for the "anti-Christ" and "mark of the beast." It was said that the virus would not infect, much less kill, people "who maintain cleanliness ... and serve God wholeheartedly. Also, the existing trust issues between Nigerians and the government made many saw COVID-19 as another conspiracy by the politicians to receive foreign financial aid and continue to embezzle them. This became further compounded by high level of denial by political leaders. For instance, a state governor was quoted in media saying "... they have been promised by God that ... COVID-19 won't get to the state." While other state governors accused the Nigeria Centre of Diseases Control (NCDC) of cooking up figures and declared zero cases on COVID-19 admission and discharged all patients even without negative test results (Olatunji O.S, Ayandele O, Ashirudeen D, Olaniru O.S (2020).

While the 5G conspiracy had limited buy-in, the Gates conspiracy resonated with deep-rooted resentment toward the West (Gagliardone, I, Diepeveen, S., Findlay, K. et al, 2021). Despite the good works done by the Bill and

Melinda Gates Foundation to eradicate polio and malaria across Africa, conspiracy theorists alleged that the foundation is out to reduce the population of Africa. Some Nigerian alleged that Bill Gates gave $10 million bribes to the National Assembly to pass a bill making vaccination mandatory for all Nigerians.

These disinformation and misinformation has made some negative impacts globally. For instance, conspiracy theory that links COVID-19 to 5G network lead to the attacks on Telecommunication infrastructure and workers (Wassens, R., 2020; Vincent, J., 2020). Furthermore, it lead to lack of trust in the government and of course, the COVID-19 control programs (Lutkenhaus, R. O., Jansz, J., and Bouman, M. P. A. (2019); Imhoff, R. and Lamberty, P., 2020), as evidenced in low vaccination and more spread of the virus (Jolley and Douglas, 2014, Wonodi, C, Obi-Jeff, C, Adewumi, F. et al, 2022).

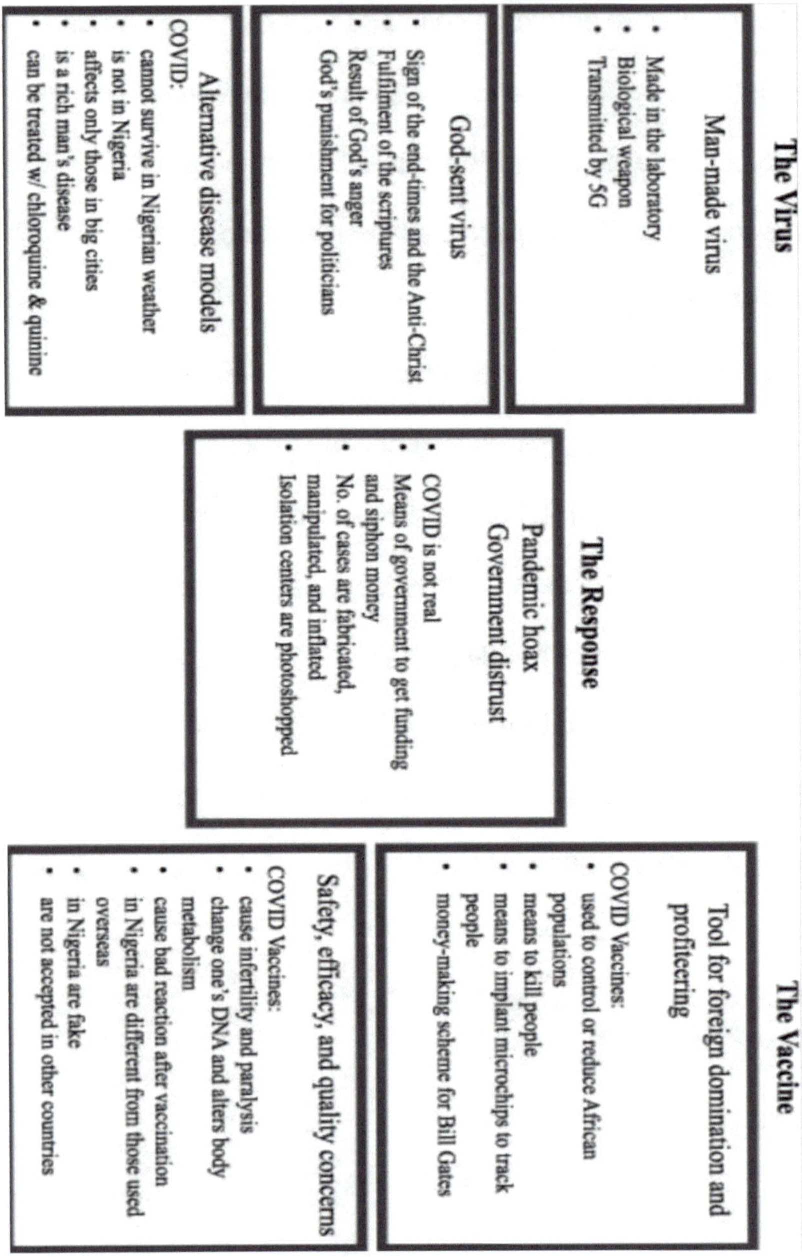

Fig. 1. Conspiracy theories and misinformation about COVID-19 and the vaccines in Nigeria (Wonodi, C, Obi-Jeff, C, Adewumi, F. et al, 2022)

Aim and Objective of the Study

The study is aimed at exploring the conspiracy theories and misinformation spread through different media in Nigeria by specifically,

i. Exploring common conspiracy theories and misinformation among respondents;

ii. Examining the extend of beliefs on the conspiracy theories and misinformation and;

iii. Seeking to understand how communication strategy can change the beliefs in such conspiracy theories and misinformation.

Methods

The study area is the Southern senatorial District of Cross River State, Nigeria. Mixed approach of both quantitative and qualitative methods were deployed for the study. Qualitative obtained through guided interview of four Key Informants (medical doctor, Clergy, Community chief and market woman leader); and Focus group discussion with 15 selected person to cut across different works of life. This discussion was guided through 6 topical areas:

i. If they believe in the existence of COVID-19

ii. What are difference knowledge and belief in the source and intentions of COVID-19

iii. Test their perception on COVID-19 vaccination

iv. Take COVID-19 precaution seriously

v. What roles does information sources play in their perceptions

vi. Obtain first hands suggestions in handling the situation

The results of the Key informants Interview (KII) and The Focus group discussion (FGD) provided the basis used in building questionnaire for quantitative survey.

A purposive sampling of 4 out of 7 Local Government Areas (L.G.As) was conducted, followed by random sampling of 100 respondents in each L.G.A to administer 400 questionnaires.

Results analyzed for descriptive statistics while contact were made with some KII and FGD for more insights, where necessary.

Results and Discussion

Demographic Information of Respondents

Description	Categories	Counts	%

Gender	Male	184	51.7
	Female	172	48.3
	Others	0	0.0
	Total	**356**	**100.0**
Monthly income (NGN '000)	≤ 50	52	14.6
	51-150	86	24.2
	150-250	96	27.0
	251-350	71	19.9
	351-450	33	9.3
	≥ 451	18	5.1
	Total	**356**	**100.0**
Age (years)	Below 21	36	10.1
	21-30	78	21.9
	31-40	97	27.2
	41-50	85	23.9
	51-60	44	12.4
	Above 60	16	4.5
	Total	**356**	**100.0**
Educational Level	Primary	28	7.9

	Secondary	48	13.5
	Diploma	97	27.2
	HND/Degree	129	36.2
	PGD/Master	43	12.1
	Ph.D.	11	3.1
	Total	**356**	**100.0**
Religion	Christianity	326	91.6
	Islam	21	5.9
	Others	9	2.5
	Total	**356**	**100.0**

Table 1: Demographic Information of Respondents

Table 1 shows the spread of respondents to cover 51.7% male and 48.3% females. Income level spread to cover the low and high income earners as well. The educational attainment of the respondents indicate that they are generally aware and educated. Almost 80% of the respondent attained at least a diploma level of education or slightly above 90% attained secondary level education. The area of study is predominantly a Christian states (91.6% of respondents). Since religious view is also essential in belief in the COVID-19 conspiracy theories, effort was made to purposively sample some Moslem (5.9%), while we have a few others (2.5%) who are mainly traditional worshipers.

Belief in the Existence and Sources of COVID-19

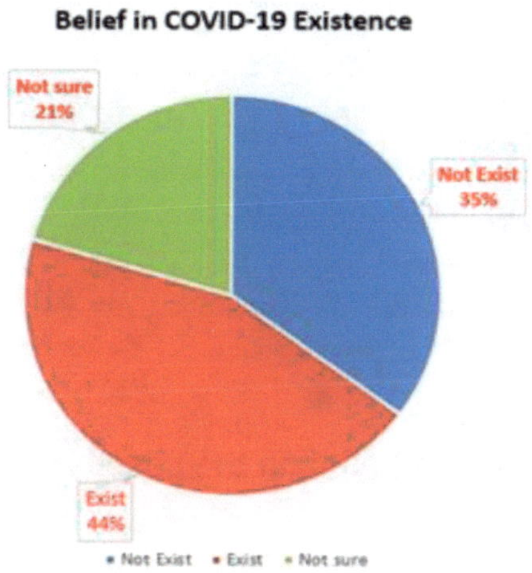

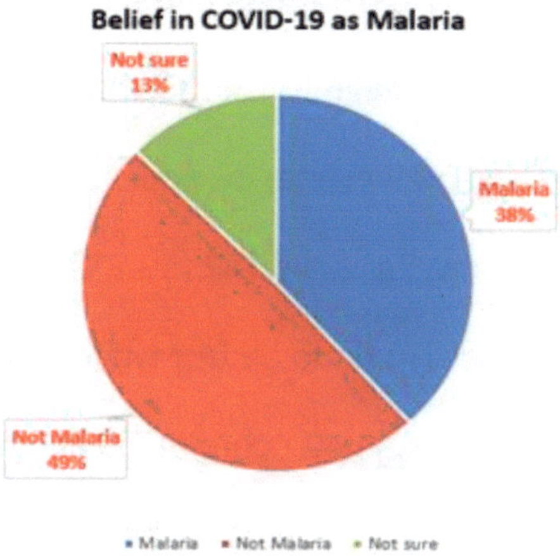

Figure 2a: Percent belief in COVID-19 existence

Figure 2b: Percent belief in COVID-19 as Malaria

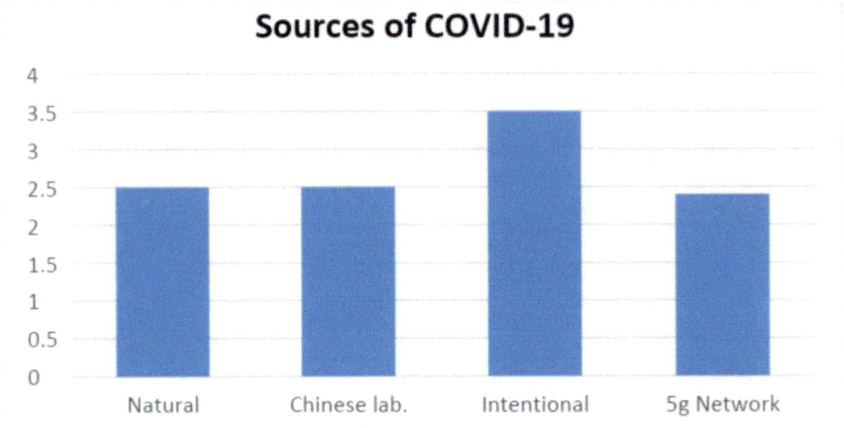

Figure 2c: Weighted scores on the belief on the possible sources of COVID-19

When asked if they believe that COVID-19 exists and the local reports that COVID-19 is only a severe variant of malaria, 125(35.1%) of the respondents do not belief in COVID-19 existence, while 158 (44.1%) believe COVID-19 actually exists- see figure 2a. Also, 142 (39.9%) believe that the COVID-19 pandemic is just a severe malaria and/or typhoid, as seen in figure 2b. Both items have overall weighted score of 2.9 suggesting that, most of the respondent are not very sure in what to believe regarding the existence of COVID-19 – more likely a gap in convincing communication. From qualitative findings, these beliefs were supported fact that the death rate from low hospitalization and death rate in the country, compared to the western nations. They believe that since we are semi-immune to malaria, they "new malaria" has less effects on Nigerians; further backed up by the social media videos where a group of doctors claimed chloroquine (Malaria drug) can cure COVID-19.

Regarding the possible origin or source of COVID-19, the respondents tend to agree more (rating of 3.5) that COVID-19 is created and intentionally released to cause the pandemic rather it being from a natural cause or accident. The cause from 5G network recorded the least score (2.3).

Conspiracy Theories and Willingness to take Vaccine

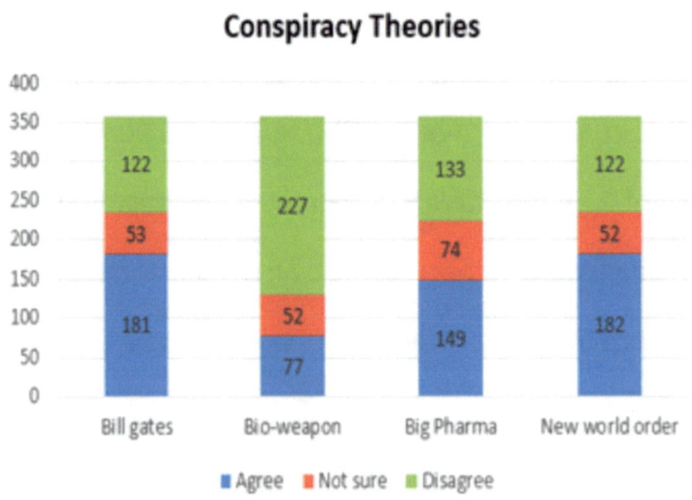

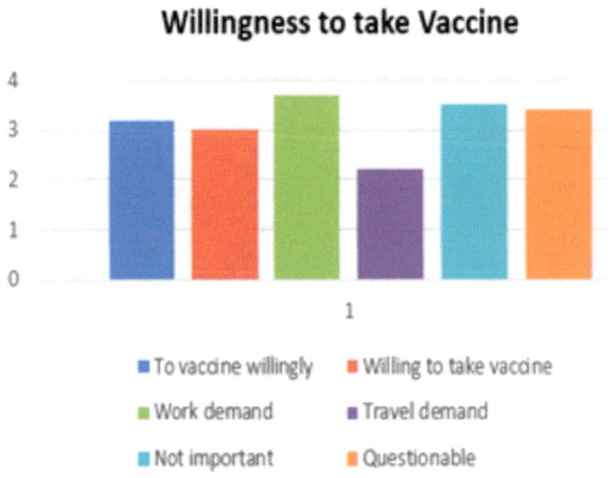

Figure 3a: Belief in Conspiracy Theories

Figure 3b: Weighted scores for Willingness to take Vaccine

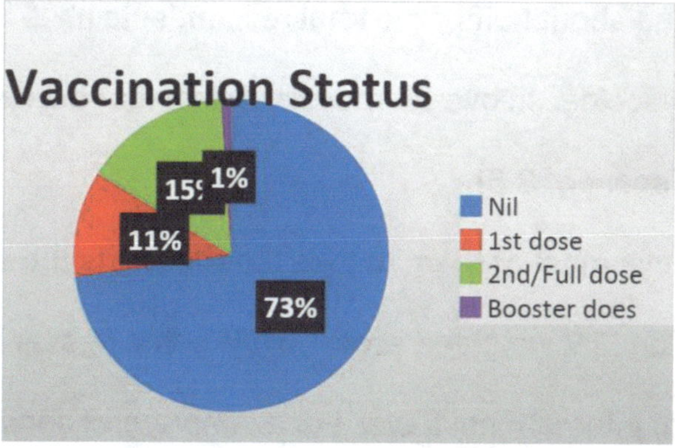

Figure 3c: Percent of Respondents Vaccination Status

As seen in the composite bar chat (figure 3a), the least accepted conspiracy theory is that of COVID-19 being a biological weapon (21.6%), followed by the belief that the big pharmaceuticals created COVID-19 for profit (41.9%). The leading belief is that Bill Gates created the virus to control African population or that some powerful individuals created it to control human race by created a new world order – 50.8% and 51.1% of the respondents, respectively, believe in these conspiracy theories.

In figure 3c, 27% of the respondent have taken at least a dose of the COVID-19 vaccine while 16% have completed the doses or have a booster dose, compare to 18TH September, 2022 national figure of 22.7% and

16.4%, respectively, from our world in data online resources (Coronavirus (COVID-19) Vaccinations - Our World in Data). Figure 3b reveals that, with a weighted score of, 3.2, a little above half of the respondents who took the vaccine did it willingly and about half of the total respondents have doubt about the safety of the vaccine. In overall, most maintain that the vaccine is not important (with a score of 3.5).

One reason that sure drove most of them to take the vaccine is the ease to access their work location (3.7 weighted score), while some (lesser score of 2.2) took if for ease of international travel. For example, civil servants during the qualitative study, claimed that the government directive of showing vaccination card before coming to work was a major drive to taking vaccine among them.

Sources of COVID-19 Information and Fact Checks

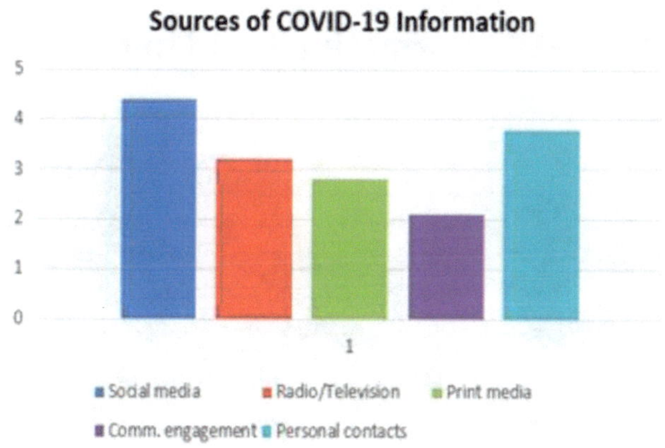

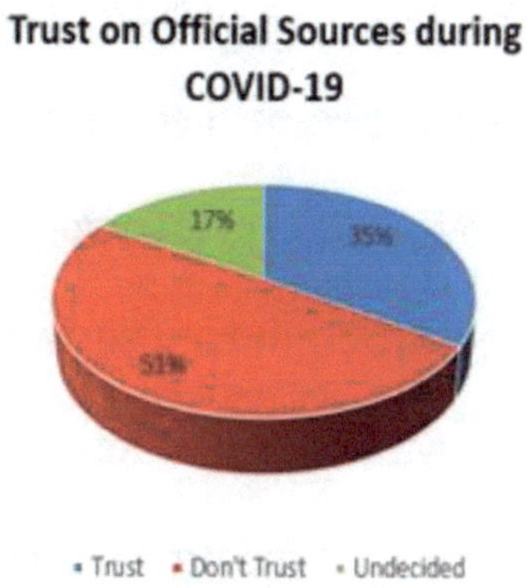

Figure 4a: Sources of COVID-19 Information

Figure 4b: Trust on Official Information Source

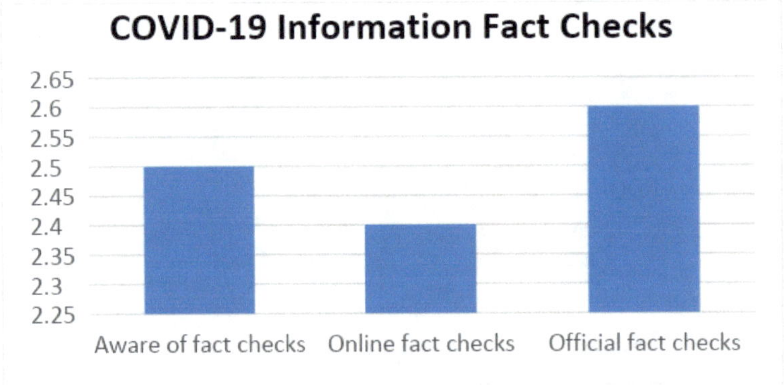

Figure 4c: Fact Checks among Respondents

As seen in figure 4a, the main source of COVID-19 information came from the social media and followed by personal contact, with high weighted scores of 4.4 and 3.8 respectively. This is followed by the traditional radio/television and print media. Community engagement and campaigns which could provide better conviction was quite low – this could be due to restriction in movement and personal contact during the pandemic. 51% do not trust official sources of information on COVID-19 as indicated in figure 4a.

Since most of the COVID-19 information came from social media, one would expect respondents to know where to confirm information. However, the respondents weighted score (2.5) indicates that most of them are not aware of the fact checking sites and consequently do not perform online facts checking (2.4), as well as not making enough necessary efforts to contact professional or official sources for confirmation (2.6). This implies that the respondents will likely use the conspiracy theories received from social media and personal contacts as bases for their perceptions about COVID-19.

Conclusion

In conclusion, respondents' belief in the conspiracy theories and misinformation is based on the predominant sources of information – social media and personal contacts. The findings support available research report that belief in conspiracy theories and misinformation tend to be less when people are exposed more to the traditional media, but is more with digital media and personal contacts (De Coninck, D., Frissen, T., Matthijs, K. et al., 2021) and that, exposure to health experts for professional information reduces belief in conspiracy theories (Humprecht, et al 2020).

Even though official channels may have tried to debunk conspiracy theories and misinformation, the approach is not effective enough, coupled with high distrust for the government officials, who sometimes contradicts their positions. This has affected the buy-in to the prevention and control program, as seen in the low willingness to get vaccinated against the COVID-19 virus and following the non-pharmaceutical preventive controls. Recommendation is for government, public health administrators and other stake holders to gear their efforts towards the design of citizens' communication model that will provide engagement at community and group levels. This will help drives penetration of scientific facts to the populace clarify questions in the mind of the citizens. This model implementation should start with government officials so as to have a common stance on what to broadcast to the public, in such critical issue as public health.

References

1. Abramowitz, S., McKune, S. L., Fallah, M. Monger, J., Tehoungue, K & Omidian, P. A. (2017) The Opposite of Denial: Social Learning at the Onset of the Ebola Emergency in Liberia, *Journal of Health Communication,* 22:sup1, 59-65, DOI: 10.1080/10810730.2016.1209599
2. Bogart L. M., Wagner G., Galvan F. H., Banks D. (2010). Conspiracy beliefs about HIV are related to antiretroviral treatment nonadherence among African American men with HIV. *Journal of Acquired Immune Deficiency Syndromes (1999)*, 53, 648–655. doi: 10.1097/QAI.0b013e3181c57dbc
3. Gagliardone, I., Diepeveen, S., Findlay, K., Olaniran, S., Pohjonen, M., & Tallam, E. (2021). Demystifying the COVID-19 Infodemic: Conspiracies, Context, and the Agency of Users. *Social Media + Society*. *7*(3), [20563051211044233]. https://doi.org/10.1177/20563051211044233
4. Geissler E., Sprinkle R. H. (2013). Disinformation squared: Was the HIV-from-Fort-Detrick myth a Stasi success? *Politics and the Life Sciences*, 32, 2–99. https://doi.org/10.2990/32_2_2

5. De Coninck D, Frissen T, Matthijs K, d'Haenens L, Lits G, Champagne-Poirier O, Carignan M-E, David M D, Pignard-Cheynel N, Salerno S and Généreux M (2021) Beliefs in Conspiracy Theories and Misinformation About COVID-19: Comparative Perspectives on the Role of Anxiety, Depression and Exposure to and Trust in Information Sources. *Front. Psychol.* 12:646394. doi: 10.3389/fpsyg.2021.646394
6. Douglas, K. M. (2021). COVID-19 Conspiracy Theories. *Group Processes & Intergroup Relations*. Volume 24, Issue 2, February 2021, Pages 270-275. https://doi.org/10.1177/1368430220982068
7. Imhoff, R., and Lamberty, P. (2020). A bioweapon or a hoax? The link between distinct conspiracy beliefs about the Coronavirus disease (COVID-19) outbreak and pandemic behavior. *Soc. Psychol. Personal. Sci.* 11, 1110–1118. doi: 10.1177/1948550620934692
8. Jolley, D., and Douglas, K. M. (2014). The effects of anti-vaccine conspiracy theories on vaccination intentions. *PLoS One* 9:89177. doi: 10.1371/journal.pone.0089177
9. Lutkenhaus, R. O., Jansz, J., and Bouman, M. P. A. (2019). Mapping the Dutch vaccination debate on Twitter: Identifying communities,

narratives, and interactions. *Vaccine X* 1:100019. doi: 10.1016/j.jvacx.2019.100019

10. Olatunji O.S, Ayandele O, Ashirudeen D, Olaniru O.S (2020). "Infodemic" in a pandemic: COVID-19 conspiracy theories in an African country. *Soc Health Behav* 2020;3:152-7. Available in https://www.shbonweb.com/text.asp?2020/3/4/152/294533. Accessed Oct 2, 2022
11. Vincent, J. (2020). *Something in the air: Conspiracy theorists say 5G causes novel coronavirus, so now they're harassing and attacking UK telecoms engineers*. New York, NY: The Verge.
12. WHO (2020). *Coronavirus disease 2019 (COVID-19) Situation Report – 86*. Geneva: WHO
13. Wonodi, C, Obi-Jeff, C, Adewumi, F, Keluo-Udeke, S. C., Gur-Arie, R, Krubiner, C., Jaffe, E. F., Bamiduro, T., Karron, R., Faden, R., (2022). Conspiracy theories and misinformation about COVID-19 in Nigeria: Implications for vaccine demand generation communications. Vaccine 40 (2022) 2114–2121

Contact information

Name of the author: Reuben Ufot Etuk
Affiliation (University): LIGS University Student
Email: reuben.etuk@gmail.com

Made in the USA
Monee, IL
05 November 2026

67813129R00122